Life on The Outside

Amy Sheppard

Life on The Outside

Women's Experiences after Leaving Provincial
Prison

palgrave
macmillan

Amy Sheppard
Memorial University
St. John's, NL, Canada

ISBN 978-3-031-63816-9   ISBN 978-3-031-63817-6 (eBook)
https://doi.org/10.1007/978-3-031-63817-6

Cover credit: © John Rawsterne/patternhead.com

This Palgrave Macmillan imprint is published by the registered company Springer Nature Switzerland AG
The registered company address is: Gewerbestrasse 11, 6330 Cham, Switzerland

If disposing of this product, please recycle the paper.

I dedicate this manuscript to the women I work with in prison and the community. It is those women who share their lives and stories with me that have made this possible. I hope this research has made me a better Social Worker and a more humble listener so that I can continue supporting and advocating for criminalized women. I am honoured that so many of you share your lives with me. Thank you to the service providers I interviewed for this project. I appreciate your insight, passion, and dedication to the people with whom you work. Thank you to the staff at NLCCW for supporting my work in the prison.

I have completed this work in St John's Newfoundland and Labrador; therefore, I respectfully acknowledge the territory as the ancestral homelands of the Beothuk and the island of Newfoundland as the ancestral homelands of the Mi'kmaq and Beothuk. I recognize the Inuit and Innu and their ancestors as the original people of Labrador. I strive for respectful relationships with all the peoples of this province as we search for collective healing and truer reconciliation and honour this beautiful land together.

A land acknowledgement is poignant, given the subject of my book. Indigenous people are disproportionately represented in the prison system, and as you will read further, Indigenous women are particularly disadvantaged and stigmatized within the criminal justice system. I want to acknowledge the many Indigenous women I have worked with over the years. One woman, who is a proud Inuk, gave me an Inukshuk key chain and a figurine because she loves to share her culture. An Inukshuk is a marker signalling that others have gone before, and we can continue in their footsteps as we make our own journey. The Inukshuk reminds me to continually bring forth the wisdom I have learned from the women I work with to the new women I encounter. Within this book, I hope to share the voices of those women who often feel voiceless—Nakummek to the women who have shared their stories.

Acknowledgements

I want to acknowledge all the guidance, patience, advice, and love I have been given through the challenging and rewarding process of writing this manuscript. I have received so much support from my partner, friends, family, colleagues, clients, and the university community.

Thank you to Rose Ricciardelli for your guidance, patience, and encouragement. You have been a source of wisdom, advice, and a critical eye to push me forward. Thank you to the team at Stella's Circle for your encouragement and support. Thank you to Katharine Dunbar Winsor, for reading and talking this project through over the years. Thank you to my family, Keith, Joanne, Lisa, and Julie, who have unwavering faith in me. Thank you to my partner in life, Shawn, who has witnessed and supported the highs and the lows and supported me in all my endeavours.

Competing Interests Dr. Amy Sheppard works for an agency, Stella's Circle, which provides services to women in provincial prison in Newfoundland and Labrador both at the Newfoundland and Labrador Correctional Centre for Women and in the community after women are released.

Ethics Approval Approval was granted by the Newfoundland and Labrador Health Research Ethics Board on August 19, 2019, Reference #2019.124. Informed consent, including consent to publish the results of the study, was obtained from all individual participants in the study.

CONTENTS

About the Author

Dr. Amy Sheppard is a practising Social Worker at a non-profit working with women in the criminal justice system. Her research and clinical interests focus on gender, criminalized women, trauma-informed practices, and critical obesity/fat studies. She teaches at Memorial University in Newfoundland and Labrador as a Per Course instructor in the Faculty of Sociology and School of Social Work.

In her spare time, she lifts heavy weights in StrongWomen competitions and dabbles in backyard farming.

CHAPTER 1

Introduction

Abstract In this chapter, I introduce the project, an exploration of desistance processes for women leaving a provincial prison. I provide context for the physical and social locations of the research. The research was conducted in an eastern Canadian province with a small population and large geography, which impacts the services provided to women in prison and upon leaving. I introduce three theoretical frameworks of desistance (cognitive, self-narrative, and social harms) used to understand how women create a life for themselves after leaving prison. Additionally, I provide a brief synopsis of the methodology used for the project and introduce the sample groups: formerly incarcerated women and service providers who work with them.

Keywords Desistance theory · Prison · Service providers · Formerly incarcerated women

© The Author(s), under exclusive license to Springer Nature Switzerland AG 2024
A. Sheppard, *Life on The Outside*,
https://doi.org/10.1007/978-3-031-63817-6_1

Ashley's Story

I want to share a story about a typical woman incarcerated in a provincial prison in Canada, the Newfoundland and Labrador Correctional Centre for Women (NLCCW). Ashley[1] is in her early twenties and served a year-long sentence for a series of shoplifting and break-and-enter convictions. She has been to NLCCW a few times for financially motivated convictions (i.e., shoplifting). Ashley is funny, smart, and a loyal friend. She participates in all activities and programmes (e.g., school, therapeutic groups, and bible study) offered in prison, and staff see her as a good influence on the other women. She completed high school while in prison and is now thinking about possibilities for future education.

Ashley's life outside NLCCW is chaos. Ashley has a drug addiction. While Percocet is her drug of choice, she will use, as she says, whatever she can get her hands on. In moments of clarity, Ashley has told me drugs numb the pain, and that is why she continues to use them. Growing up, her family was neglectful, and they, too, had problems with substance abuse. Ashley did not have a stable family life as a young girl. Therefore, with little family protection, she was raped and assaulted. As an adult, Ashley has had violent relationships with boyfriends. She is in love with the father of her child, who is controlling, abusive, and in prison. Her child was removed from her care and adopted. The loss of her child continues to be a raw wound. While in prison, Ashley does not use drugs, so all the pain from her experiences floods her senses. She has flashbacks, panic attacks, nightmares, and disassociates. She has moments of rage that she struggles to control.

Yet, with all these challenges, Ashley is able to participate in prison programmes and has goals for when she leaves prison. She would like to continue the schooling she started while in prison. She would like to work and have a family. Ashley is tired of a lifestyle that has brought her to prison multiple times and wants to make some changes. However, she is not sure how she might make these changes. She feels like she has little family or friend support to help her stay away from her criminal lifestyle. She worries about where she will live on release from prison. She fears returning to drug use, which fuels her chaotic lifestyle. She has asked me and other professionals for help.

---

[1] All names of interview participants are pseudonyms.

Ashley's story is typical of many women in provincial prisons throughout Canada. Incarcerated women tend to be young, poor, under-educated, and underemployed. Most women in Canada's prison system have experienced multiple traumas and substance abuse/misuse. Their crimes tend to be related to survival, engaging in minor thefts or fraud to meet their needs. Women often engage in crime due to histories of abuse, trauma, substance use, and mental health concerns. These issues can lead to criminal behaviours for survival, connecting the blurred nature of victimization and offending. For many women involved in the criminal justice system, involvement with crime is wrapped up in an attempt to cope with abusive histories and is a survival strategy.

Let's consider the name of the institution where Ashley has been living for a year: a *correctional* centre for women. What does this name imply? In the case of a "correctional centre," correction means rehabilitation. I want to start from the assumption that prisons, at least in part, have a goal of rehabilitation, whereby a person has the opportunity to address criminal behaviours so as not to commit another crime (Ward & Maruna, 2007). Thus, one of the focuses of rehabilitation is that prisoners do not return to prison. Beyond rehabilitation is the goal of desistance, a process by which people disengage from criminal activity and move towards a pro-social lifestyle (Weaver & Weaver, 2013). Ashley and many other women like her are interested in committing to a life of desistance. They do not want to return to NLCCW. They want to engage in a crime-free life. However, as I explore throughout this book, desistance is not easy.

Desistance is a process. Nugent and Schinkel (2016) suggest that the process of desistance is not linear. Rather, desistance involves periods of engaging in criminal activity, refraining from criminal activity, identity shifts, and recognition of change by others. Furthermore, a person's environment, community, and society will affect their desistance journey. An individual's hope for desistance is, in part, dependent on the recognition by others as a "non-offender" (Nugent & Schinkel, 2016, p. 580). Said another way, the more support an individual receives in shifting from a criminal to a pro-social identity, the more likely the individual is to sustain desistance. Framed by desistance theory, I interviewed formerly incarcerated women and service providers working with formerly incarcerated (and incarcerated women) to learn their thoughts about the process of desistance and what they believe can support the process.

I think about Ashley, a typical woman serving time at NLCCW. How might her experiences in prison shape her ability to desist from criminal activities and meet her goals? What does she need when she is released from prison to support her in desistance? Ashley is an example of many women who serve time in a short-term provincial prison, and the questions apply to all of these women. This book explores the experiences of 16 women released from prison and how their time at NLCCW impacted their goals and eventual desistance from criminal activity. In addition to these 16 women, I have also interviewed service providers who work with criminalized women both in the community and prison to enhance the picture of how desistance processes can work for women leaving a provincial prison in Canada.

CONTEXT OF THE STUDY

Women from Newfoundland and Labrador (NL) serve provincial sentences (less than two years) and are remanded to NLCCW located in Clarenville, about two hours outside St. John's, the province's capital. The Centre has the capacity to house 28 women.

While often, the public assumes that prisons house those who have been convicted of crimes, most people in provincial prisons are on remand. Meaning, they have been charged but not yet convicted of a crime and not released on bail before trial. Women are often remanded to prison because they are homeless or they lack family resources that would enable someone to act as a surety for their release. Being remanded often means planning for release is difficult due to being unsure when a woman will be getting out of prison. Often, women appear in court for sentencing and get time served, meaning they are released from court there and then with no planning or support. Challenges related to remanded prisoners are one of many issues in supporting women released from NLCCW.

Another issue is that most women from this province serve their sentences far from their home communities. While women will be released from NLCCW and return to their home communities throughout the province, the majority of women will return to the St. John's area, the capital of the province. The vast distances from home communities mean that women often do not have visitors while incarcerated. Furthermore, release planning is challenging when community resources are far away. Making connections to community recourses while inside prison is invaluable in providing continuity of care for women on release (Fortune et al., 2010). The location of the prison impacts community-based agencies' abilities to provide those reach services that are needed.

Furthermore, several disturbing issues have plagued NLCCW and the treatment of women involved in the criminal justice system over the years, including overcrowding, inadequate resources for Indigenous women and deaths of incarcerated women.

There has been a rise in admissions, causing overcrowding. Thus, in 2016, the Department of Justice and Public Safety decided to modify a section of the men's prison facility known as Her Majesty's Penitentiary (HMP) to house 14 women. The government framed the decision to move women to Her Majesty's Penitentiary as a temporary measure (CBC, 2016). While the overcrowding situation at NLCCW has not been consistent, there have been several times when the section for women at HMP has been closed and reopened. Overcrowding of the prison means that there is not enough physical space to house women. At times, women are triple bunked in a cell, meaning one woman is on a mattress on the floor. The prison is a small space; therefore, tensions among the women run high when it reaches or overflows maximum capacity. There are few spaces for retreat away from others within the institution. Furthermore, overcrowding challenges abilities to provide adequate programming to all women due to limited space.

In addition to overcrowding conditions at NLCCW, there have been serious concerns about the treatment of Indigenous women involved in the criminal justice system within NL. Like the rest of Canada, in NL, Indigenous women are over-represented in the correctional system and face many challenges due to race, geography, and language. Some of the challenges identified for Indigenous women include racism from other prisoners and feelings of loneliness and isolation. Furthermore, Innu and Inuit women are often "lumped" together by staff without acknowledging the differences and occasional clashes between these two groups (Sheppard, 2016). A further barrier for Indigenous women at NLCCW is language. English is not the first language for some women from small coastal communities, which makes it challenging to provide programming and services (Sheppard, 2016).

Most Indigenous women in prison come from Labrador and are very far from home. On release, their journey home includes the two-hour bus ride to St John's airport and an hour-and-a-half-long flight to Goose Bay. From there, many women will then continue to smaller coastal communities. On the other hand, a correctional facility for men in Labrador offers culturally specific programming and is closer for family visits. Indigenous female prisoners from Labrador do not have access to the same services as Indigenous men serving prison time.

Tragically, in 2018, two women suddenly died while incarcerated at NLCCW. In the same year, two men died while incarcerated in the men's prison. These four deaths resulted in a review of services provided within the prisons. Jesso (2018) concluded that numerous issues within the prison systems contribute to poor mental health among those housed in prisons. She posited that the lack of physical space to provide adequate programming and services led to the inability to meet the security and health needs of prisoners. Recommendations include new prison facilities, updated training for correctional officers, increased programming and services for those living in prisons, and more integrated health care services. Some of the recommendations have been implemented with plans to implement more, including building a new prison to replace the current infrastructure.

While there are serious concerns about prison systems within the province, there are some bright spots. As I discuss in later chapters, there are several services with NLCCW that women report as being helpful and addressing their mental health concerns. Furthermore, there are dedicated staff in the institution and in communities working with broken systems to address the needs of women housed there. I count myself as one of those staff working with women to support them as best I can.

My place within this research is immersive in that I am both working as a researcher and as paid employment as a Social Worker in NLCCW as a part of the Just Us Women's Centre which is a part of Stella's Circle. Stella's Circle is a non-profit based out of St. John's, NL. The organization works with marginalized individuals who struggle with mental illness, homelessness, addiction or criminal justice involvement. Various programmes in the organization provide services to help people meet goals such as employment, safe and secure housing and feeling a sense of belonging in our community. The Department of Justice and Public Safety contracts the Just Us Women's Centre to provide services to women at NLCCW and in the St. John's area.

I have worked as a social worker with the Just Us Women's Centre since 2009, when the programme began. Our programme provides services to criminalized women both within the prison and in the community. Community-based services include therapeutic group and individual counselling, social/recreation activities, and concrete supports (accessing housing, clothing, hygiene products, and access to phones and computers). Prison-based services include therapeutic group work, individual counselling, and supporting prison staff with release planning.

Given these dual roles, as a researcher and social worker, I am invested in working with women leaving prison. I have been thinking a lot about my role as a storyteller in this research. In my social work position, I feel like I am a storyholder, a storykeeper. People tell me things, and I keep their confidence. People tell me stories of trauma and abuse, stories about shame, joy, anger, and lust. All kinds of stories about all kinds of parts of life: people tell me stories that make me laugh with them. People tell me stories where I have to hide my reactions and feelings. I have heard stories that make me angry, make me empathize, and that I cannot get out of my head. These are stories I cannot always tell. Nevertheless, these are stories that have become a part of me. These stories are a part of my soul because they connect me to deep parts of humanity.

However, now I have moved into a researcher role, with permission to tell stories. I am asking for stories, and people tell me their stories with the permission that I will share. Sharing stories is important. Other people have already told these women's stories. For example, local news sources often tell women's stories based on crimes committed, rarely asking women for their perspectives. Women are often embarrassed by how the news stories portray them. These stories live on through Google and are easily searchable, ensuring that some women re-live one-sided stories.

I, too, will tell a story because stories matter. Hearing "layered" diverse voices over time and space contributes to understanding the experiences of people, particularly marginalized people (McAleese & Kilty, 2019). Also, importantly, how I tell the stories matters. I feel responsible for telling the stories I hear because some stories need to be heard. I have a place of privilege and power that enables my voice to be heard. Thomas King believes that stories are medicine, "a story told one way could cure, that same story told another way could injure" (King, 2008, p. 14). Women have trusted me with their stories with an intention to share with other women, with service providers and with others in an effort to seek a "cure," which is improving the lives of criminalized women. So, it is with humility that I share the stories of 16 women here and countless others who have shared their stories with other service providers and me.

In my role as a social worker, during a group in prison, I facilitated an exercise whereby everyone secretly wrote something nice to everyone else in the group. One of the women in the group wrote to me, sharing that I am one of the reasons she is considering sobriety. While I know that it is not me, personally, encouraging her to consider sobriety, it is my role as a social worker to which she is responding. However, this was a significant moment for me. It can be challenging to work in a prison environment when your role is to help people change where so many women return. It is challenging to work in and be a part of an oppressive penal system. I have spent much time reflecting on my role as a social worker working within systems that are often focused on punishment and shame (see Sheppard, 2019; Sheppard & Beausoliel, 2019). As a social worker and now as a researcher, I want to provide a little something that helps. Thus, my interest in researching desistance. Every day, I see that women want to make changes in their lives and struggle to do so, and I want to help support those changes.

I want to be clear that while my research focuses on women who want to move away from a criminal lifestyle, some criminalized women may not be interested in making changes to their lifestyle or may not be in a position to do so. These women, who may not be on a path towards desistance, deserve understanding, support, and compassion. Kendall (2020) demands that feminist allies do not require "respectability" from women who have had to "face hard life choices" (p. 4). In my position as a social worker, I can see some of these "hard life choices" and am privileged to hear from women about their lives. My research informs my social work practice with individual women who want to make changes. In addition, my research has also informed my social work practice aimed at social justice and challenging structural inequalities for all criminalized women, not just those who seek to make changes to their criminal lifestyle.

DESISTANCE THEORY

I use desistance theory to understand how women think about their release from provincial prisons. Desistance is, simply put, a process whereby an individual moves away from crime and towards a pro-social lifestyle. Women in the current study have engaged in the process of desistance, but their journeys have not been simple. Therefore, I examine their experiences through the lens of three theoretical considerations to elucidate their experiences through the desistance process,

I look first at theories that emphasize the individual's cognitive processes, Giordano and colleagues' (2002) theory of cognitive transformation and Maruna's (2001) theory of self-narrative. In addition, I also explore theoretical understandings of desistance that challenge the focus on individual change and centre systemic issues impeding women's desistance efforts. Barr (2019) reconceptualizes desistance as a move away from androcentric ways of looking at desistance and towards a critical desistance framework which can centre women's lives.

Cognitive Theory of Desistance (Giordano et al., 2002)

Giordano and colleagues (2002) identify a four-stage cognitive process in the movement towards desistance. First, the individual must be open to change (e.g., the individual tires of their old lifestyle and desires "going straight"). The second stage is exposure to a "hook." A "hook" may be a job, school, a relationship or anything else that creates a positive development in the life of the desister. The combination of the person's willingness to change and the attitude towards the "hook" fosters desistance. Thus, it is not just the job offer that provides an impetus to lead a life of desistance. One needs to want to live a crime-free lifestyle, invest in the job, and believe the job is meaningful and contributes to a crime-free life.

The third stage of cognitive transformation in the process of desistance is envisioning a replacement self (e.g., a new pro-social version of themselves). The shift in identity is vital in allowing for new cognitive constructs that encourage the person to think about themselves as someone who does not engage in criminal behaviour. Once established, the new identity guides desistance behaviours (i.e., a criminal lifestyle is no longer compatible with the new identity). Thus, the "hook" begins the process of creating a new identity, and "a solid replacement self may prove the stronger ally of sustained behaviour change" (Giordano et al., 2002, p. 1002).

The final stage in cognitive transformation is how the desister views their former criminal lifestyle. The "capstone" of the process of change is when the desister no longer sees their old criminal behaviours as "positive, viable, or even personally relevant" (Giordano et al., 2002, p. 1002).

Theory of Self-Narrative: (Maruna, 2001)

Maruna (2001) offers a desistance theory suggesting that for a criminally involved person to "go straight," they must generate a gradual shift in self-narrative. He states that the narrative of desisters differs from those active in a criminal lifestyle in three fundamental ways: (1) the establishment of core beliefs that characterize "true self," (2) an optimistic view of having control over their future, and (3) a desire to be productive and give back to society. Those who can "rehabilitate" generate a positive self-narrative that states that they are still good people even though they have done wrong, often reaching back to find the positives in the "old me." Thus, Maruna (2001) argues that desistance is not merely something that happens to a person but is an active process.

Social Harms Approach (Barr, 2019)

Giordano and colleagues (2002) and Maruna's (2001) desistance theories posit that desistance is possible when individuals with criminal histories make fundamental cognitive shifts. Feminist criminologists have critiqued theories highlighting cognitive shifts for their emphasis on the individual while ignoring the social processes that may impede an otherwise willing desister (Barr, 2019; Comack, 2018; Hart, 2017; Sered, 2020). These scholars point to women's histories of poverty, trauma, and mental health/addiction issues that can be the pathway for women's criminal activity as a continuing barrier to women's desistance. In essence, the question is, how do women desist from crime when the very pathways to crime continue to create problems in women's lives?

Barr (2019) argues for a "critical desistance lens," which must ground desistance research and practice within the structural conditions in which desistance does or does not occur when considering women's desistance processes. She argues that women's experiences of desistance can mean challenging gender norms, just as deviance often does. For example, research indicates that becoming a mother is a significant desistance-inducing social bond for women who break the law (Bersani et al., 2009; Giordano et al., 2002; Uggen & Kruttschnitt, 1998). However, Barr (2019) found that for most women in her study, criminal activity happened *after* becoming a mother and was often related to providing for children. Barr (2019) challenges the traditional notion that women require stability, for instance, with their children and husbands, for successful desistance. Instead, in her study, she found that desistance was a largely independent venture, meaning that women in her study avoided romantic relationships, at least temporarily. Thus, for Barr (2019), desistance stories can be seen as resilience and survival in the face of "normal" (patriarchal, neo-liberal, heteronormative) expectations such as marriage and family.

Further, Barr (2019) argues that researchers working with criminalized women must question the conditions in which their criminalization, punishment, and post-criminal justice system contact occur. She articulates a social harms approach, whereby she reimagines desistance. Barr (2019) sees desistance not as a concept that involves a move away from crime but as a concept that involves a move away from harm, whether these harms are interpersonal (violence, trauma) or from relations with the state (inadequate mental health services, poverty).

Methodology

To understand the reentry and desistance processes for women released from prisons in NL, I conducted interviews with two groups: formerly incarcerated women and service providers who work with these women both in the community and in prison. I elected to interview these two groups because each provides insight into the challenges and what might work within the reentry and desistance processes for women leaving prison and returning to the St John's area. Interviewing formerly incarcerated women aids in understanding the challenges of transitioning from prison back to the community from their unique perspectives, as each woman has a different experience.

Service providers have experience working with numerous criminalized women and can provide a wealth of information from working with a diverse population. There is a dearth of research examining service providers' experiences in working with criminalized women. However, they can provide a wealth of information due to their own experiences as they support their clients and engage in their emotion management strategies to engage in their work (Dunbar Winsor, 2023). Service providers who work closely with criminalized and imprisoned women can provide their perspectives on the challenges of providing services to women on reentry, including systemic barriers. Furthermore, examining service providers' perspectives can aid in understanding how services have been designed and provide local context for what is available to this population. Thus, interviewing these two key groups provided a rich data source that complemented each other and provided diverse experiences.

Interviews were informal, using a semi-structured interview guide. As I knew most of the interviewees through my work as a service provider or as colleagues working in the same field, interviews were conversational in style in that there was discussion back and forth. However, qualitative interviews have an asymmetrical power relationship between the interviewer and the interviewee. While the interview seemed conversational in style, I led the questions asked, and therefore, the conversation can be seen as a one-way dialogue (Brinkman & Kvale, 2015). Given the power imbalance due to my position as a social worker and the nature of research interviews, I allowed the interviewee to ask me questions, which I answered. Furthermore, I turned off the recorder at their request, allowing the interviewee some control over the interview.

Interviews, however, differed from my usual work interactions with clients because I asked questions related to a particular topic rather than areas necessitated by my work obligations. For example, in my professional work, conversations are about helping clients understand their feelings/life/situation during counselling sessions. By contrast, in research interactions, interviews were open-ended yet maintained focus with directive prompts and questions. I entered into the interviews wanting information on reentry and desistance experiences, yet I listened to interviewees' stories that diverged from the specific topic of my interest. In essence, I always prioritized the interviewees' voices. Interviews were semi-structured, meaning I had a list of questions. Nevertheless, there was an openness to the sequence of the questions (Brinkman & Kvale, 2015). This interview style allowed conversational paths to emerge organically and emphasized the participants' voices as their ideas led the interview.

Formerly Incarcerated Women Sample

I conducted 16 interviews with formerly incarcerated women who had returned from NLCCW to the St. John's area. I asked about their release from prison, specifically, factors that helped and those that would have helped with desistance. I also solicited their perspectives on how women in prison struggle to change and move towards a crime-free lifestyle. I asked women about their future goals, including what they wanted for themselves in the next few years. These questions helped elicit "change talk," highlighting how women view desistance processes (Maruna, 2001).

Women interviewed were from all over NL but had moved to St. John's, many as a way to access more services. The length of time since incarceration varied from a couple of days after incarceration to 15 years. The lengths of sentences also varied. For example, one woman spent a few days in the lock-up before being released on house arrest. Another woman spent eight years in prison between remand at NLCCW and her eventual sentence of four years at Nova Institution for Women. The ages of women interviewed ranged from 21 to 79, and two self-identified as Indigenous. The other 14 women self-identified as white.

Service Provider Sample

I interviewed 16 service providers, asking about the types, quality, and access to services available to women within and after leaving prison. In addition, I asked them to describe what they have observed about policies and practices for criminalized women and how such policies and practices could improve. My conversational interviews with service providers examined barriers in community connections such as employment, mental health services, and housing.

All service providers were based in St. John's, although some organizations provide province-wide services. They worked with marginalized populations who experience mental health and addiction issues, homelessness, poverty, and racism and are often street-entrenched and have high needs.

Service providers had a range of tenure in the field, from two years to 21 years. All service providers had earned a bachelor's degree, with some having degrees in specialized fields such as Social Work or Occupational Therapy. The services offered varied. Some service providers perform prison in-reach as a regular part of their job, while others work with women post-release. While not all service providers were mandated to work specifically with criminalized women, the types of service provided meant that criminalized women used these services.

In the following chapters, I examine what formerly incarcerated women and service providers who work with them believe is needed to support women's desistance journey post-prison. Chapter 2 explores the relationship between desistance and recovery from substance use. For many women involved in the criminal justice system, substance use is common and connected to criminal involvement. I assert that women see their recovery from substances and desistance from crime as the same process. Further, I highlight how women have used their prison experiences to begin their journey towards desistance and recovery.

In Chapter 2, women share that their desistance journey begins inside prison, often through detoxing from substances, which allows for clearer thinking.

Chapter 3 explores women's experiences post-release and focuses on housing needs. There is a dearth of housing options for women post-prison, and women in this study reflect on how they navigated housing options post-release. Services providers, too, weigh in on how women can be supported through safe housing post-prison. Building on the foundation of housing, Chapter 4 examines how women think about the services they need to support their desistance. Women interviewed have asserted that they need more of the good services that are available to them, as they assert that the bad services need to be improved upon through gender-responsive and trauma-informed practices.

Chapter 5 highlights the stigma that criminalized women face when attempting their journey towards desistance. Finally, I end the book with a reflection on what we can do better to support women navigating the tumultuous path of their desistance journeys.

REFERENCES

Barr, Ú. (2019). *Desisting sisters*. Springer.

Bersani, B. E., Laub, J. H., & Nieuwbeerta, P. (2009). Marriage and desistance from crime in the Netherlands: Do gender and socio-historical context matter? *Journal of Quantitative Criminology, 25*(1), 3–24.

Brinkmann, S., & Kvale, S. (2015). *Interviews: Learning the craft of qualitative research interviewing* (Vol. 3). Sage.

CBC. (2016, March). 'Desperate measures': Spike in female inmates proves prison system is not working, expert says. Retrieved March 8, 2024, from https://www.cbc.ca/news/canada/newfoundland-labrador/hmp-women-1.3472259

Comack, E. (2018). *Coming back to jail: Women*. Fernwood Publishing.

Dunbar Winsor, K. (2023). *"Wading against a tide": Emotions, ethics and the interstitial space of community service provision for criminalized mothers* (Doctoral dissertation, Concordia University).

Fortune, D., Thompson, J., Pedlar, A., & Yuen, F. (2010). Social justice and women leaving prison: Beyond punishment and exclusion. *Contemporary Justice Review, 13*(1), 19–33.

Giordano, P., Cernkovich, S. A., & Rudolph, J. L. (2002). Gender, crime, and desistance: Toward a theory of cognitive transformation. *American Journal of Sociology, 107*(4), 990–1064.

Hart, E. L. (2017). Women prisoners and the drive for desistance: Capital and responsibilization as a barrier to change. *Women & Criminal Justice, 27*(3), 151–169.

Jesso, M. (2018). *Newfoundland and Labrador correctional and community services: Deaths in custody review.* St. John's: Department of Justice. Retrieved February 29, 2024, from https://www.gov.nl.ca/jps/files/publications-pdf-death-custody-review.pdf

Kendall, M. (2020). *Hood feminism: Notes from the women that feminism forgot.* Viking Press.

King, T. (2008). The art of Indigenous knowledge. In Knowles & Cole (Eds.,) *Handbook of the arts in qualitative research* (pp. 13–25). Sage.

Maruna, S. (2001). *Making good: How ex-convicts reform and rebuild their lives.* American Psychological Association.

McAleese, S., & Kilty, J. M. (2019). Stories matter: Reaffirming the value of qualitative research. *The Qualitative Report, 24*(4), 822–845.

Nugent, B., & Schinkel, M. (2016). The pains of desistance. *Criminology and Criminal Justice, 16*(5), 568–584.

Sered, S. S. (2020). Beyond recidivism and desistance. *Feminist Criminology, 16*(2), 165–190.

Sheppard, A., & Beausoliel, N. (2019). A delicate dance: Towards an embodied social work practice. In S. Frigon & C. Apotheloz (Eds.), *Dancing around the world—Towards resilience and social justice [Danser autour du monde—Vers la résilience et la justice socials]* (pp. 139–156). University of Ottawa Press.

Sheppard, A. (2016). *Making up our own moves: Exploring, movement, dance and experiments of the body at the Newfoundland and Labrador Correctional Centre for Women* (Master's Thesis, Memorial University).

Sheppard, A. (2019). Reflecting on rehabilitation: A practitioner's point of view. *Journal of Community Corrections., 28*(3), 7–12.

Uggen, C., & Kruttschnitt, C. (1998). Crime in the breaking: Gender differences in desistance. *Law & Society Review, 32*, 339.

Ward, T., & Maruna, S. (2007). *Rehabilitation: Beyond the risk paradigm.* Routledge.

Weaver, A., & Weaver, B. (2013). Autobiography, empirical research and critical theory in desistance: A view from the inside out. *Probation Journal, 60*(3), 259–277.

CHAPTER 2

Planning While Inside: Desistance and Recovery

Abstract Criminalized women have high rates of substance use, which are often related to their criminal activity. This chapter explores how women think about the impacts of prison on substance use and their journeys to recovery. Some women share that prison can be helpful in their recovery, seeing prison as a proxy detox. Women interviewed see their substance use as something out of their control, and thus, prison provides the structure to remove themselves from their substance use. I find that women interviewed for the study see recovery from addiction and the process of desistance as the same journey. Meaning that when they refrain from substance use, criminal activity will cease.

Keywords Substance use · Recovery · Agency · Change · Desistance and addiction

INTRODUCTION

In Canada, criminal activity and drug/alcohol use are connected in ways that include criminalizing some drugs, such as those considered "hard drugs" like cocaine and heroin. The criminalization of some drugs can lead to criminal charges such as possession of or trafficking of illegal substances. However, even those substances considered legal, like alcohol,

© The Author(s), under exclusive license to Springer Nature Switzerland AG 2024
A. Sheppard, *Life on The Outside*,
https://doi.org/10.1007/978-3-031-63817-6_2

can contribute to illegal behaviour (i.e., driving while impaired). In addition, substance use is indirectly related to crime. Some people engage in criminal activity to obtain drugs or while under the influence of substances. Young and colleagues (2021) showed that more than 42% of Canadian crimes resulting in a custodial sentence between 2006 and 2016 would probably not have occurred if the perpetrator had not been under the influence of or seeking alcohol or other drugs.

Incarcerated women have high rates of substance use in Canada. Correctional Services Canada (CSC) staff assessed federally sentenced women and found that for 47% of women in the study, their crimes were related to their substance use (Farrall MacDonald, 2014). Furthermore, women in prison are up to 10 times more likely to have a drug addiction than women in the general population (Fazel et al., 2006; Henderson, 1998). In their study of provincially sentenced women, Buchanan and colleagues (2011) found that 82% of participants self-identified as substance users. At my place of work, 90% of women we work with report substance misuse before entry into provincial prison.

Women I interviewed see recovery from addiction and desistance from crime as the same process. While drug use is not a crime, participants believe their addiction and criminal activity are linked such that once the addiction stops, crime will also cease. Furthermore, some women in the current study stated that addiction led them to prison. For instance, Jane shares, "I started getting in trouble after (a loss in my family). I got into drugs, selling drugs, doing drugs and keep my habit going, and then I went in (NLCCW) (month redacted) of last year." As illustrated here, women see addiction, not criminal activity, as the cause of problems in their lives. The majority of women in the current study, 12 out of 16, connect their criminal behaviour to substance use. Either they committed a crime in pursuit of obtaining the substances (i.e., shoplifting to pay for drugs), or they committed a crime while under the influence of substances (i.e., assaults committed while intoxicated). During interviews, I asked women what changes they wanted to make when leaving prison to help ensure they did not return to prison. All women with addiction issues stated that they wanted to stop alcohol/drug use as they believed that was the cause of their entry into criminal activity and prison. From these conversations, I propose that women see recovery from addiction and desistance from crime as the same process.

Throughout the current chapter, I use the term addiction because it is the word participants use to describe their problematic substance use. For women, the word addiction implies a loss of control over their substance use and, further, a loss of control over their lives, ultimately leading to a prison sentence. Therefore, substance use is not merely substance use or misuse for participants. More accurately, the addiction becomes their life in that women spend all their time trying to obtain or using drugs/ alcohol. Jane shared, "Something clicked in my head that I'm done with that life." She means that she no longer wants to continue the cycle of drug use and criminal activity that had consumed her for five years. Jane and other women in this study inextricably link recovery from addiction and desistance from crime, meaning that no longer using alcohol or drugs means no more criminal activity.

In this chapter, I share formerly incarcerated women's experiences with addiction and how they see their addiction as connected to desistance processes. In addition to women's voices, I will also impart experiences of service providers working with criminalized women and how they see addiction affecting women's lives. I explore four themes connected to recovery from addiction and how recovery interacts with desistance processes. First, many women see their prison sentence as the beginning of the recovery process, viewing prison as a proxy rehab/detox. Given that prison can be the first step in recovery from addiction for some women, I explore the barriers to recovery and treatment options when leaving the prison system. I then present women's agentic view of change: they state, "You have to want it." Women uttered this phrase repeatedly during interviews when asked about the process of change, placing the individual at the centre of any change. Said differently, even if there was easily accessible treatment on every corner, to make change happen, *you* have to want it. Finally, I examine women's views of their future. I connect each of these themes with the desistance process woven throughout women's recovery narrative.

PRISON AS DETOX/REHAB

Nine of the twelve participants who identified addiction as a problem stated that going to prison helped with their recovery. Three women did not find prison helpful in recovery. I speak to their experiences a little later in the chapter.

In addition to what I heard from women in this study, in my work at the provincial prison, women talk about how prison can be helpful in providing a safe space from drug/alcohol use, homelessness, or violent partners. I frequently hear from women that they would likely die from drug overdose without prison providing a break from substance use. For these women, the prison was a forced detox that allowed them to abstain from substances when they felt unable to abstain on their own or as would be experienced in a more traditional detox programme where clients have the option of leaving. Monica shared, "I was out, and I wanted to go back there (to prison). It was my choice to go back there and want to do all the time (meaning, complete her sentence in prison). It is kind of sad when it reaches that point, though." Monica had been at NLCCW on remand before her release to the community on house arrest. She wanted to return to prison, feeling that prison was the only way she could "dry out" from substances. Monica elaborates that her reality is "sad, though," implying that she could not abstain from substances on her own. She felt deeply that her addiction was extreme and out of her control. For Monica, prison helped control her drug use, given their limited access at NLCCW. Monica's choice to complete her sentence in prison rather than on house arrest is her first step towards desistance and recovery; she began the process of openness to change (Giordano et al., 2002). While in prison, Monica asserts she chose to abstain from drugs and deal with her addiction issue; she was open to change and ready to work towards recovery from addiction and desistance.

It is not uncommon for illicit drugs to find their way into a prison (Jesso, 2018; Mullaly, 2011, 2017) or for prisoners to misuse prescribed medication (Tamburello et al., 2017). At NLCCW, occasionally, drugs enter, but not in amounts large enough to sustain a long-term drug habit. Prisoners, on occasion, do attempt to misuse prescribed medication. They either "hoard" the medication prescribed, trade it to other women, or save enough for a high. On the one hand, Monica describes prison as a place that forces her to give up her substance use, providing structure and motivation when she lacks control. However, Monica has more agency and control over drug use than she credits herself; she chooses to stay away from the illicit trade. Prison provides the structure she cannot receive elsewhere but needs for her addiction despite making positive choices towards recovery and desistance.

Monica shared that prison as a method of detox was helpful. Further, more than merely providing a space to avoid substances, most women stated that their prison time helped them "get clean[1]" and, thus, "clear their head." For example, Gloria stated, "to be cleared of everything (alcohol and drugs) and be sitting there for those two and a half months. It made me realize that you do need help. Okay. You got a problem." Gloria was on remand for two and a half months before her release to a sentence of house arrest. Prison let Gloria abstain from drugs and alcohol use, allowing her to think about her life and what may require change. She recognized that alcohol and drugs were a problem and that she needed help to address her addiction. She was able to make a plan to maintain sobriety after leaving prison and develop further life goals, including her return to school. According to Gloria, the impact of a "clear head" helped her think without the influence of substances, thus shaping her cognitive processes in her desistance journey.

For Monica and Gloria, prison served as a proxy detox/rehabilitation centre, representing the essential physical component of detoxing. After detoxing, women see themselves as no longer physically impacted by the drugs. In recognizing that drugs and alcohol "clear" their system, women feel they can think without the impact of drugs on their cognitive function. Clear thinking means they can make plans for change for the first time in a long time, including recovery from addiction and the criminal lifestyle that accompanied their drug/alcohol use. The idea of a "clear head" is critical to cognitive-based desistance theories. Without the ability to clearly conceptualize a new identity and lifestyle—to formulate a position for the future—the desistance process will not work.

While prison may help some women, like Monica and Gloria, detox from substances, it is not an easy process. Robyn shared that she used prison as an opportunity to abstain from substance use and make plans for her future. However, she stated that it was difficult to stay in a recovery mindset when other women in prison did not have the same goals. Robyn lamented that some women attended groups because they were bored or to get the incentives offered for attendance at groups:

---

[1] I recognize the problematic nature of the term "clean" when referring to abstaining from substance use. The Editorial Team for *Substance Use* suggests refraining from using slang and idioms such as "clean/dirty" when talking about substance use. However, they also encourage more research and consultation with individuals affected by drug and alcohol use (Broyles et al., 2014). Given that "clean" and "clear" are the terms used by the women interviewed, I honour their voices and use their words.

> You hear them (other incarcerated women) in the meetings or in groups or therapy or whatever. The thing was, as soon as the workers are out, you guys (service providers) are gone or whatever, and it goes back to normal, they're just shit-talking it, or you know. What I mean is they don't take any of this seriously.

For Robyn, hearing that other women did not take recovery and the work involved in therapeutic groups seriously was discouraging and made her question her own recovery goals. Monica also shared that it was challenging to hear other incarcerated women talk about their plans to use drugs when released. Recovery from addiction is not a solitary process and often involves reaching out to others in the recovery community for support and encouragement. Thus, for some women in prison who felt that others around them were not engaged in similar recovery-oriented goals, the recovery process was difficult and isolating.

On the other hand, many women expressed that connection to community and peers can provide a sense of spirituality, which is vital to the desistance process. Many women reported having feelings of peace, calm, and community when attending groups. While imprisoned, women spoke about needing to find meaningful activities to engage in both in and outside prison. I wrote in my research journal about a shift I needed to make in my thinking about what women in prison need after introducing a creative writing group:

> An "othering" that happens in empathy for marginalized, vulnerable women. Like they are still not 'like' us. In recognizing my privilege, I often assume that women in prison will not be "into" stuff like journaling, vision boards, collage- it seems like bullshit when there are more urgent needs. But they love these activities when presented. Yes, we need bread, but we need roses, too.

Women in prison responded with great enthusiasm to the creative writing group when I doubted it would be of interest. I believed that women would focus more on basic needs such as readying housing and income for release from prison. However, women were able to find meaning through poetry and short stories in their prison experiences that helped them in cognitive transformations and moves towards desistance. In my journal, I referenced the Bread and Roses strike, whereby women fought for fair wages and decent working conditions, with the belief that women needed their basic needs met, but they also needed to have some of the good things in life that make life worth living (Ross, 2013). I see this as accurate for women in my study as well. The path to desistance is mired when basic needs are unmet, but women also need roses, good things in their lives, to make desistance a worthwhile endeavour.

As I assert the need for roses, fun, and meaningful experiences while in prison, we must not neglect basic needs. Robyn felt that the lack of support in release planning impeded her plans for release. Robyn stated she was committed to sobriety while in prison and planned to stay sober when released. However, she criticized the lack of help actualizing plans at release. She spent much time making plans, writing goals, and adhering to what she learned in therapeutic groups. However, her preparation was for naught when she was released without safe, sober living arrangements. Robyn was released from prison to live with a former boyfriend, who was supportive but with whom she used drugs and alcohol. Living with her former boyfriend, who used substances, caused her to return to alcohol and drug use, which led to criminal behaviour, although she did not return to prison. Robyn is currently in recovery and is proud to state that she is no longer under any court order, having desisted successfully for several years (in fact, she is working on getting a record suspension! This is an amazing achievement and seemed out of reach for Robyn at the time of her incarceration.) However, she believes her recovery process would have been smoother and without relapse had she been able to leave prison for safe, sober housing.

Vivian, who has been working as a service provider, echoes Robyn's thoughts about the lack of planning. Vivian worked with people who have had challenging housing histories. She has worked with many people released from prison into homelessness. In her experience, most released women are committed to working on their recovery and want to desist from crime. Vivian stated that most of her clients saw prison as a place to detox, to get "clean," and a place to think about new goals. She believes prison could be a good time to work with clients to teach coping skills and help them develop goals if they are in a "good headspace." However, if inadequate supports are in place for when the person is released from prison, work inside prison is fruitless. I had a detailed conversation with Vivian about supports in and out of prison:

> Vivian: It's an absolutely good opportunity to teach people skills and talk about other ways that their life could look. But unless you have services that are going to be available as soon as

	people are released to help them practice those skills in the real world because you can't practice them in jail. You can practice a little bit, but you're not going to have…
Amy:	It's not the real world. It's a safe place to practice it…
Vivian:	It is, but unless you have the support, can you practice and stuff once you're out? To me, it's the same as any kind of treatment without follow-up care. Yeah, and you got to learn how to use the stuff in your real environment, especially if you're going back to the stuff you left. Yeah, and if you've got added stressors. Like, you know, there's a lot of stress. I mean, obviously, being incarcerated a stressful in many ways. But there's also a lot of things that you don't have to worry about when you're incarcerated. You don't have to worry about food, or you know, your medication or …
Amy:	Even just basic safety for a lot of women like (Vivian: 100%). You know, as much as I know, prison can be a dangerous place. But it's often more dangerous at home, especially for women.
Vivian:	I think that's it. I think the services that follow people's incarceration need to line up with what people actually did while they were incarcerated. Like any programming that people learn, needs to flow into community, right? So you can't have people teaching something or have programming on the inside and discharge planning that doesn't match up with what's actually going to happen when they get out. I think it needs to be very intensive initially and outreach-based with a focus on finding safe and affordable housing for people as quickly as possible and continuing on with like practicing and using skills once they get out.

My conversation with Vivian highlights problems within the rehabilitative model of prison. Both formerly incarcerated women and service providers interviewed acknowledged that there is help within NLCCW. Women stated that the services are meaningful and of good quality. They stated that prison can help clear their mind and teach them new skills to help them on the path to recovery. However, Vivian points out that when prison programming, discharge planning, and community living do not align, the recovery and desistance process derails. Vivian's ideas are consistent with Ricciardelli and colleagues (2019), who found that releasees who participated in programming while in prison felt that programmes did not transfer into the community on release.

For some female prisoners, prison can be a temporary refuge from their marginalized lives in the community (Bucerius et al., 2021). Further, the women I interviewed thought about prison as potentially a time to learn new skills, gain insight into the self and begin a process of change towards a pro-social life. Women in the current study expressed openness to changing their criminal lifestyle. As per Giordano et al.'s (2002) cognitive theory of desistance, they engaged in "change talk," meaning that women used words indicating the desire to change. Change talk included conversations about new people in their lives, goals for the future, and distancing from bad influences and positive activities such as starting school or sober socializing. All women stated they did not want to be involved in the criminal justice system. Instead, they desired to live a new, "normal" life, including meaningful relationships, employment, and a safe place to call home and connect to the community.

Giordano et al. (2002) suggest that openness to change is a basic need for a cognitive shift, but exposure to a hook for change is central to desistance. The hook can be a job or a relationship but must be meaningful to the individual, influencing them to see a positive shift in their lives. Giordano et al. (2002) suggest that the hook is an integral part of the desistance process because it focuses on "the relationship between actor and environment" (p. 1001). Women in the current study did not speak about what might be considered powerful hooks, such as a job or marriage. In fact, many women in the current study suggested that their environment did not change on release from prison and indicated that returning to the same environment challenged their ability to desist. For example, women reported a lack of safe and sober housing on release from prison. They reported experiencing stigma when trying to find employment. They reported unsupportive family and friend networks. Nevertheless, women were still able to engage in the process of desistance.

I suggest that their current environment did not provide the hook for women in the current study. Instead, the hook was a vision of a future "normal" life, including a supportive family, a job, and a safe place to live. For the women I interviewed, the hook is not readily available but is a vision of possibilities for the future. Some women had pieces of a vision of a "normal life," such as meeting new friends, which makes obtaining the full vision of a normal life seem achievable. However, a hook, in the traditional sense, was not readily apparent. Without supports in place to help those who want to change work through some barriers, the time spent working on themselves feels futile.

Not all interviewed women with addiction issues stated that prison was helpful in their recovery. Some acknowledged that prison wasn't helpful but didn't believe that prison made their addiction problem worse. On the other hand, one woman was explicit that prison did not help but was, in fact, harmful to her recovery and mental health. Judy was sentenced to a prison term on old charges, meaning that she had committed the crime years ago, and the court system was not immediate in her sentencing. Being sentenced for an older charge means that for Judy, her life was severely disrupted. She stated, "I can say I went there (to prison) sober, straight, working, had my apartment all lovely." While Judy was able to keep her apartment to return to on release from prison, she does not feel prison provided any rehabilitative help to support her already crime-free life. Judy stated that she was "a recovering alcoholic" when she went to prison, and she did not receive any treatment or support in her recovery. She described being treated inhumanely, comparing the prison to a concentration camp, and as a result, her mental health deteriorated while in prison. I asked Judy if she felt worse off for being in prison. She stated, "No, not worse, but like Joan of Arc, saying, something in there has got to change." Judy was able to channel her anger at being in prison towards something productive. She was able to advocate for increased treatment for women in prison. Judy was in prison over 20 years ago when no formal therapeutic programming was in place. Interviewees who had a more positive experience were able to avail themselves of therapeutic programming related to addiction, in part due to Judy's advocacy.

Thus, for Judy, prison paused the desistance process already underway. Before prison, Judy lived as her "replacement self," she was working, had an apartment, and lived a crime-free lifestyle. Judy's experience of imprisonment affected her mental health, making her feel worse about herself. However, Judy stated that she came out of prison "a fighter," meaning that her prison experience did not cause her to fall back into old behaviours. Judy's desire to help other women in prison fits with Maruna's (2001) understanding of desisters who desire to be productive and give back to society. Judy was released from prison into her desistance-focused life with a new meaning and purpose: to help other women in prison.

BARRIERS TO RECOVERY AND DESISTANCE

All participants experiencing addiction sought treatment for addiction in various forms, both in prison and in the community. Three women used self-help groups such as Alcoholics Anonymous or Narcotics Anonymous. One woman sought treatment through the NL health care system, which offers in-patient and out-patient treatment. Ten women stated that they preferred services offered by non-profits, such as those with Stella's Circle. Two Indigenous women stated that they benefited from traditional healing-based cultural practices. Finally, one woman stated that she was able to abstain from drug use on her own by keeping active in school and her social life, including social-based programmes offered at non-profits. She did not seek any formal addiction treatment. While women were engaged in various activities and treatments to varying degrees, they did highlight several barriers to recovery from addiction. Service providers also shared barriers they have encountered when advocating for treatment services for clients. Barriers include a lack of safe housing and waitlists for treatment. I examine each below.

Safe and Sober Housing

There is a lack of affordable, safe housing for women when they leave prison. Housing issues also arose when women spoke about their struggles with addiction. Many women spoke about being released and "going back to the same place." For example, Robyn returned to live with an ex-partner with whom she used drugs. She stated that she tried to abstain from drug and alcohol use, but it was difficult while living with someone who continued to use. Another example is Beth, an Indigenous woman, who shared that she wanted to return to her home community but that it is hard to be in a community where there is a lot of alcohol and drug use. She states:

> I just feel, like, because back home is just a lot of alcohol and too much. I've heard since I been in jail like there used to be a lot of people smoking weed. But now they don't do that. There's people selling coke there, and I don't want to be going, to be a part of that. I don't want to be around it. And I know that's hard. Yeah, and drinking, for me that was the biggest addiction. Yeah, I don't like to be around it.

For Beth, returning home is important; her family, community, and culture are at home. However, she also knows she is returning to a place where drug and alcohol use is common. In fact, Beth heard that cocaine, arguably a more dangerous drug, has replaced marijuana. Hearing about the introduction of cocaine in her community worries Beth because she does not want to be involved with "harder drugs." Furthermore, there is limited housing in her home community, meaning that Beth will have to live with family members who use alcohol and drugs. She does not have the opportunity to have her own place, which could provide a safe haven in her community amidst the issues she identified.

On the other hand, "going back to the same place" can also mean generally going back into an unsafe community and living environment. For example, while Gloria and Monica did not return to the same communities or homes, they worried about returning to the same lifestyles. Gloria left prison and went to a friend's home, which she quickly left as drug paraphernalia was visible in the apartment. Monica left prison and went to a different community to escape drug-using friends. She says:

> If I went back to (location redacted), the same things would happen—same crowd. I needed to go to a different location, and you're used to your groups; you're used to your support (that I had in prison). So I might as well make a fresh start, right?

However, she was homeless on release and had to go to a shelter. Being released to a shelter was scary for Monica because she was in an unfamiliar community. Nevertheless, Monica believed that she needed a "fresh start" in a place where she knew no one to continue with the recovery process she started while in prison.

Beth, Monica, Gloria, and Robyn are all engaged in the cognitive process of desistance. They are trying to distance themselves from their old life, as exemplified by Beth stating, "I don't want to be around it," and Monica refusing to return to her hometown. Monica is beginning to envision her replacement self as she undergoes "a fresh start." She sees all that can be different for her, even in prison, where she engaged in therapeutic groups and support. She knows she can be supported on release. Monica, Robyn, and Gloria were also trying to distance themselves from their pasts by finding new places to live, but all struggled to find safe, sober housing.

For all these women, safe, sober housing is crucial to recovery when released from prison. Without a safe, sober home, seeking treatment seems futile, impeding the recovery and desistence processes. Women are returning to unsafe housing, and communities can encourage the resumption of a lifestyle that links criminal activity and addiction.

Waitlists

Another barrier to continuing recovery on release from prison is the waitlists for treatment centres. Several service providers identified that waitlists for treatment are problematic, as people need to access treatment when they are ready and willing to go. Delays in treatment may mean that people slide back into drug/alcohol use and, for interviewees, also returning to a criminal lifestyle. Willingness to go to treatment is openness to change, the first step in the desistance process described by Giordano and colleagues (2002). Therefore, assisting women in attending treatment would be beneficial on the journey to desistance. Jackie, a service provider, shares what she believes would help women on release from prison:

> The ability to not be on this long waitlist for treatment. So that when you think you're clean, when you've been not using because you've been incarcerated for six months, and you get out, and you want to continue that, and so treatment is where I'm going, but there's a long waitlist. So, trying to then you get back (to your home community), and you may end up using again, which can further delay getting into treatment.

Jackie sees that women in prison are serious about recovery from addiction and want to access treatment centres when released. However, waitlists often mean that there is no seamless transition from prison to an in-patient treatment facility. Jackie sees this transition as a critical component to supporting women's recovery efforts because they often return to places where drug and alcohol use is common. Moser et al. (2015) suggest that the continuity of care model, as suggested by Jackie, is an effective method to support any treatment efforts made while in prison. Ruby, a service provider, shared evidence of this model working within her programme. She works in a treatment setting whereby released prisoners are mandated to participate as a condition of release. I asked her about some of the challenges in working with criminalized women, to which she replied:

> I don't see it as any different than anybody else, aside from the obvious that they have conditions that apply while they're here because of their correctional sentencing. So sometimes (we are) a little bit more strict. I don't see that as a deterrent, though, because it can help people stay on track, especially if they have addictions because sometimes, we know that external influence can help people get to a place where they start to internalize their reasons for wanting change. So, yeah, I don't see that as a deterrent. I think that's actually helpful for some women,

Ruby's words reveal that, in her experience, an external influence, such as parole, can encourage people to think about their reasoning for making a change. Her view is consistent with former prisoners who described the prison as a detox space, an opportunity to think and make changes. However, Ruby extends women's assertion that prison is a proxy detox/rehab centre to include community-based treatment programmes. She suggests that women can continue the recovery process and desistance in the community under supervision, which can be helpful. Ruby's work exemplifies how continuity of care can extend from the prison into the community.

AGENTIC VIEW OF CHANGE

When talking about changing their addictive and criminal behaviour, women consistently stated, "You have to want it." "Wanting it" fits with cognitive theories of desistance, which view desistance as a cognitive and deliberate thought process rather than something that just happens. Interviewees see themselves as the agents of change in their lives. Laura, a formerly incarcerated woman, states, "It is in yourself to make a change. No one is coming knocking on your door, asking if you want help. You have to take that first step." Laura sees that help is available but that the individual must be the agent of change. Likewise, Jane said, "You guys are there and are good. But we have to do the work." Both women see value in reaching out to professional supports and help, but ultimately, they believe they are responsible for making changes in their lives. Thus, their addiction is individualized into a personal problem rather than a community or societal issue.

In their study with persisters, Kang and Kruttschnitt (2022) found that the importance of the agentic self was overstated, meaning that the individual's will did not always override difficult situations, leading them back to a life of crime. Nonetheless, women in this study strongly believed that it was a personal responsibility to make change. Thinking about their responsibility to make change fits with neo-liberal visions of empowerment, which insist that women are responsible for their well-being (Elfleet, 2022). This neo-liberal approach dismisses the lived realities of criminalized women and women in this study who are often caught up in patriarchal, colonialist, and heteronormative structures, which create vulnerabilities and marginalization in their lives (Rutter & Barr, 2021). However, while women engage in neo-liberal ideas of responsibility, it is important to listen to how they internalize that responsibility. In the face of systemic issues that throw up barriers, stigma, and violence, women see themselves as empowered to make changes within their lives.

Women's views of themselves as agents of change in their lives fit Maruna's (2001) theory of desistance, whereby desisters maintain an optimistic view of control over one's destiny. Most women stated they have been able to take charge of their lives with a plan, including long-term goals, such as employment and children, and everyday schedules that include fun and social activities. Katie shared:

> It's just.... there's so much more out in the world, and my God, yeah. I was in a basement for so many years. Never seen the sunlight. Until like this year. So I had an amazing summer. The best one in so long. I had a group of people like. We did everything. Just go and have bonfires; just go....We used to go on hikes up somewhere off the highway. It would kill us. (laughter) You couldn't breathe. Yeah, we did everything, went bowling, went swimming. Movie nights. Out with the kids swimming. Just every day, we're doing something.

For Katie, she is taking charge of life by participating in daily, fun activities that she missed out on in the past due to her lifestyle. Likewise, Monica has a daily routine that helps her "manage." She explains:

> Well, I mean, you are going to school, and you're out and then, you're gone for a walk. You're keeping yourself active, and by the time you go home and you clean up. You tired, right? It's time for bed.

These women take charge of their lives and live the "normal," quotidian life that many women identify as their goal. Their lifestyle is new and thus, the feeling of taking charge to live "normally" feels empowering.

Young (1994) has defined empowerment as "the development of individual autonomy, self-control, and confidence and/or the development of a sense of collective influence over social conditions in one's life" (p. 49). For women in this study, empowerment is the first part of the definition, the start of developing self-control and self-confidence in their ability to take charge of their lives. They are missing the second half, a sense of collective influence over the social conditions of life. The women interviewed often did not recognize that social contexts can limit their ability to make choices, no matter how much they want. Certainly, women recognized that they were poor and that employment with a criminal record and being a woman would be challenging. However, they internalized the idea of self-responsibility in terms of their addiction/criminal lifestyle. The internalization of self-responsibility can be problematic as women often do not see that the system has failed them but rather see themselves as the failure. That can be challenging to the recovery and desistance process that relies on feelings of optimism and mastery over one's destiny (Maruna, 2001). In these cases where women internalize self-responsibility, it is helpful for service providers to introduce the Social Harms approach to desistance (Barr, 2019). Helping women to contextualize their experiences of desistance within systems that marginalize their experiences and impede their progress may help women to understand that they are not entirely to blame if they slip or relapse into substance use or criminal behaviour.

Service providers can step in to support women's journey towards desistance and recovery. Service providers certainly see systemic barriers, such as poverty, that impede women's successful desistance. Pearl, a service provider, envisions a more welcoming and supportive community for women with additions. She shares what she would like to see:

> I guess it would be great to see more options for people who are struggling with addictions or substance use. So more housing for those people. More programs for those people. More recovery centers for those people that are really low barrier. Really supportive. Less criminal charges for those people. Like I know, it's complicated. More fucking..., even like parks. We

need better schools. We need more resources for things like education and Creative Expressions and art and those kinds of things.

Those are all kind of like, in my opinion, things that help enrich people's lives and build a stronger sense of community so that people are less inclined to or when they do get engaged with things like substances or violent relationships or whatever. It may be they are less isolated, or they're less inclined to just kind of keep it in and like continue to re-enter that cycle. Yeah, the more likely they are to kind of engage in a community and engage with each other and build friendships. And like I said, that opening up. Kind of less like I'm a fucking victim, and I am like wounded, and I can't break this and more like I'm open to like whatever comes next.

Pearl has several ideas to support women with addiction issues, which address a sense of belonging to a community. Importantly for Pearl, too, is for women to feel empowered and "open to whatever comes next." Service providers' roles are to advocate for women and help them see that if they do "fail" at recovery or desistance, it is likely a systemic failure and not necessarily the woman's.

Envisioning the Future

The journey towards desistence means envisioning a replacement self after exposure to a "hook." A "hook" may be a job, school, a relationship, or anything else that creates a positive development in the life of the desister (Giordano et al., 2002). The hook for interviewees was what they considered a "normal life." Sophie stated, "I want to stay healthy, stay strong. I want to see my grandkids graduate with their high school." Laura says, "I wanted things better. Yeah, I want a better life, a regular life. Not a drug-using life." Gloria shared, "My current goals are just to be the best mom... getting a better education, getting back into the workforce." Katie stated her goals were to get her driver's licence and that she "plans on getting my trade. My apartment is my first thing." These are achievable, modest goals for a "normal life," working, family, and an apartment—the "hooks" for desistance that can lead women to seek addiction treatment and move towards desistance.

These goals for a "normal life" are reasonable and achievable. However, many women also shared the challenges in obtaining such a life once they are "clean." Because addiction and criminal lifestyles are so enmeshed, women expect that once they stop using substances, life will be manageable and "normal." However, some normalcy, such as obtaining a job, is not easy. Furthermore, women also noted that abstaining from substances exacerbated symptoms of mental disorders because they have been self-medicating. Women noted increased anxiety, depression, and symptoms related to potentially psychological traumatic event exposure. Most women in prison have experienced exposure to trauma and often drug/alcohol use how they cope (Covington, 2011; Matheson et al., 2015). For example, Katie shared, "I have dealt with some trauma as a child, which led to my drug use, I guess. I have been kind of numbing my pain since I have been 15." Thus, abstaining from drugs and alcohol means that women have to feel what they have been numbing (Loucks, 2004; Richie, 2001). This "hook" of quotidian, "normal" life does not always live up to its promise for some women. Women are still likely to live in poverty even after recovery. Women are likely to experience stigmatization due to their past, including struggles with family relationships and difficulties with employment. While the hook may be disappointing, most women can still reach the final stage, seeing their old selves as no longer viable.

Some interviewees believe that their criminal activities and their addiction are the same behaviours. Therefore, they saw the prison as a proxy detox, a way of taking a first step on the path to recovery and desistance. Other women I spoke to did not see prison helping with their substance use but rather added to their pain. The key is to understand for whom prison is a turning point and for whom it is a source of continuing disadvantage. Understanding women's differing responses to prison is key to those working as service providers within the criminal justice system. Understanding the differing responses can guide a work plan for each woman.

For some women interviewed, drug/alcohol treatment is the first step towards desistance. Obtaining treatment indicates a willingness and openness to change, as Giordano et al. (2002) described. Interviewees saw prison as helping with that first stage of treatment. Many stated that prison enabled them to "get clean," clearing their head as they began the process of desistance and a lifestyle change. The openness to change leads women to see the next stage in the process, which is the hook. A "hook" may be a job, school, a relationship, or anything else that creates a positive development in the life of the desister. The combination of the desisters' willingness to change and the attitude towards the "hook" fosters desistance (Giordano et al., 2002).

Women also struggle to find their identity but know they are not the same as they were. The struggle in finding a new identity is where service providers and therapists who understand this process can help by helping to create a replacement self. Women need support in working through symptoms of trauma exposure and mental disorders. They need support in identifying goals for employment and schooling. They need advocacy for housing and employment so that life can be a little easier and "normal."

Interviewees explain that recovery from addiction means not coming back to prison. Women see recovery and desistance as synonymous. Van Roeyen and colleagues (2017) suggest that recovery and desistance are dual processes related through a dynamic interplay. They caution against researchers conceptualizing desistance and recovery as the same process. As a researcher, I separated the concepts of recovery and desistance; however, women in this study see these processes as one. Desistance is enmeshed in the recovery process because women's lives are complicated and not easily separated into discrete behavioural parts. Many women inextricably link crime and addiction, and they believe crime will cease once they are in active recovery.

Kang and Kruttschnitt (2022) found that drug use greatly impacted study participants' ability to engage in desistance. Colman and Vander Laenen (2012) similarly found that people engaged in both recovery from drug use and desistance felt that desistance resulted from recovery. In their study, respondents described recovery as coming first. While in my findings, women state that crime will cease once their addiction is under control, for them, recovery is, at least in part, "not coming back to jail." A significant difference may be the idea of "going back to jail," as in the Colman and Vander Laenen (2012) study, participants did not have an incarceration history. The cognitive shift imperative in desistance processes involves re-thinking the future self and distancing from the past self. For interviewees, the past self is an "addict" who used drugs and/ or alcohol, but also, the past self is a "criminal" who engaged in criminal actions required to obtain drugs.

Furthermore, prison is a significant addition to a past identity beyond criminal activity, whereby "not going back to jail" is a vital piece of distancing from the past. The future self is seen as "clean," meaning not using problematic substances² and not being imprisoned. Thus, for women, recovery and desistance appear to be the same process.

Conclusion

In the research journal I kept throughout this project, I wrote about a woman at NLCCW who told me that coming to prison saved her life. She had been in a substance use treatment centre but left, returning to using drugs and drinking. While under the influence of alcohol, she committed a serious and dangerous crime and was happy that she was sent to prison. She believed that prison was the only thing that would save her because she could not leave and use drugs or alcohol. She told me that she was thinking clearly for the first time in years.

It can be hard to hear when women tell me that prison saved their lives. Prison is not a pleasant place. They are living in an institution with few comforts. They are far from family and friends. Nevertheless, women deeply entrenched in addiction state that they need a place that they cannot leave to survive and for eventual recovery. That does not mean that punishment is what they want (or need). It does not mean that they should not have access to family or services or decency or comfort. It means that they need to "get away" to recover. For women deeply entrenched in addiction, going to prison is a surrender of control. Women seek security (in the warmest sense of that word), and ironically, prison is where they can find security. As Davis and colleagues (2022) state, we need to work alongside prisoners while advocating for their release. I advocate that while prisons exist, we need to provide good quality care and services for the people who live there. Furthermore, we need to ask why women are stating that some aspects of prison are good. The question becomes, what do we need to do in our communities to enhance services so that these women get what they have said they get in prison?

Interviewees believe that desistance and addiction are inextricably linked, such that when I asked about desisting from criminal behaviour,

---

² Most women do not aspire to abstain from all substances. Most women see problematic drug use as opioids, cocaine and alcohol. Many women state that they will continue to use marijuana. This is in keeping with a harm-reduction approach to addiction, which posits that complete abstinence from substances is not always feasible, and thus, reducing the harmful impacts of problematic behaviour is the best approach in supporting people's recovery.

they talked about recovery from addiction. For them, recovery does not come first; desistance and recovery from addiction are the same things. Many women shared that prison was the first step towards change as it allowed them to detox from drugs and think clearly. By no means are recovery and desistance easy processes. There remain barriers to living pro-social lives, yet women have managed to live the "normal" lives they have set as goals for themselves. The fact that women recover from addiction and desist from criminal activity is a testament to their motivation for change and desire to "want it." Despite systemic barriers, women interviewed see themselves as agents in their destiny. They "want it," and they get it.

References

Barr, Ú. (2019). *Desisting sisters*. Springer.

Broyles, L. M., Binswanger, I. A., Jenkins, J. A., Finnell, D. S., Faseru, B., Cavaiola, A., & Gordon, A. J. (2014). Confronting inadvertent stigma and pejorative language in addiction scholarship: A recognition and response. *Substance Abuse, 35*(3), 217–221.

Bucerius, S., Haggerty, K., & Dunford, D. (2021). Prison as temporary refuge: Amplifying the voices of women detained in prison. *British Journal of Criminology, 61*(2), 519–537.

Buchanan, M., Murphy, K., Martin, M. S., Korchinski, M., Buxton, J., Granger-Brown, A., & Martin, R. E. (2011). Understanding incarcerated women's perspectives on substance use: Catalysts, reasons for use, consequences, and desire for change. *Journal of Offender Rehabilitation, 50*(2), 81–100.

Colman, C., & Vander Laenen, F. (2012). "Recovery came first": Desistance versus recovery in the criminal careers of drug-using offenders. *The Scientific World Journal, 2012*, 657671.

Covington, S. (2011, October). *Trauma matters: Changing the world without work*. Paper presented at the 14th National Conference on Adults and Juvenile Female Offenders.

Davis, A. Y., Dent, G., Meiners, E. R., & Richie, B. E. (2022). *Abolition. Feminism. Now* (Vol. 2). Haymarket Books.

Elfleet, H. (2022). Neoliberal feminised governmentality: The role and function of a post Corston Report (2007) women's centre in the north-west of England. *British Journal of Community Justice, 16*(2), 1–22.

Farrell MacDonald, S. (2014). *Lifetime substance use patterns of women offenders* (RS 14-24). Correctional Service of Canada.

Fazel, S., Bains, P., & Doll, H. (2006). Substance abuse and dependence in prisoners: A systematic review. *Addiction, 101*(2), 181–191.

Giordano, P., Cernkovich, S. A., & Rudolph, J. L. (2002). Gender, crime, and desistance: Toward a theory of cognitive transformation. *American Journal of Sociology, 107*(4), 990–1064.

Henderson, D. J. (1998). Drug abuse and incarcerated women: A research review. *Journal of Substance Abuse Treatment, 15*(6), 579–587.

Jesso, M. (2018). *Newfoundland and Labrador correctional and community services: Deaths in custody review.* Department of Justice. Retrieved February 29, 2024, from https://www.gov.nl.ca/jps/files/publications-pdf-death-custody-review.pdf

Kang, T., & Kruttschnitt, C. (2022). Can persistent offenders help us understand desistance from crime? *Journal of Developmental and Life-Course Criminology, 8*(3), 365–392.

Loucks, N. (2004). Women in prison. In G. McIvor (Ed.), *Women who offend* (pp. 142–158). Jessica Kingsley Publisher.

Maruna, S. (2001). *Making good: How ex-convicts reform and rebuild their lives.* American Psychological Association.

Matheson, F., Brazil, A., Doherty, S., & Forrester, P. (2015). A call for help: Women offenders' reflections on trauma care. *Women & Criminal Justice, 25*(4), 241–255.

Moser, A., Matheson, F., Grant, B., & Weekes, J. (2015). Treating addictions in correctional settings. In M. Herie, W. Skinner, & G. Maté (Eds.), *Fundamentals of addiction* (pp. 461–479). Centre for Addiction and Mental Health.

Mullaly, R. (2011). 'This has been a huge mistake.' *The Telegram.* Retrieved February 24, 2024, from https://www.saltwire.com/newfoundland-labrador/news/local/this-has-been-a-huge-mistake-125881/

Mullaly, R. (2017). Smuggling drugs inside Kinder surprise to HMP inmate lands woman two-year jail term. *The Telegram.* Retrieved May 24, 2021, from https://www.saltwire.com/newfoundland-labrador/news/local/smuggling-drugs-inside-kinder-surprise-to-hmp-inmate-lands-woman-two-year-jail-term-129942/

Ricciardelli, R., Sheppard, A., & Mooney, T. (2019). Employment reentry: Unpacking the experiences and recommendations of former federal Canadian prisoners. *Advancing Corrections: Journal of the International Corrections and Prisons Association, 7*, 97–112.

Richie, B. E. (2001). Challenges incarcerated women face as they return to their communities: Findings from life history interviews. *Crime & Delinquency, 47*(3), 368–389.

Ross, R. J. (2013). Bread and roses: Women workers and the struggle for dignity and respect. *Workingusa, 16*(1), 59–68.

Rutter, N., & Barr, U. (2021). Being a 'good woman': Stigma, relationships and desistance. *Probation Journal, 68*(2), 166–185.

Tamburello, A. C., Kathpal, A., & Reeves, R. (2017). Characteristics of inmates who misuse prescription medication. *Journal of Correctional Health Care, 23*(4), 449–458.

Van Roeyen, S., Anderson, S., Vanderplasschen, W., Colman, C., & Vander Laenen, F. (2017). Desistance in drug-using offenders: A narrative review. *European Journal of Criminology, 14*(5), 606–625.

Young, I. (1994). Punishment, treatment, empowerment: Three approaches to policy for pregnant addicts. *Feminist Studies, 20*(1), 33–57.

Young, M. M., De Moor, C., Kent, P., Stockwell, T., Sherk, A., Zhao, J., Sorge, J. T., Farrell MacDonald, S., Weekes, J., Biggar, E., & Maloney-Hall, B. (2021). Attributable fractions for substance use in relation to crime. *Addiction, 116*(11), 3198–3205.

Housing: Where Do I Go After Prison?

Abstract Women leaving prison often have limited housing arrangements on release. This chapter discusses some challenges in securing housing for women leaving prison in NL. Both formerly incarcerated women and service providers explain challenges to housing and share what they believe is needed so that women are supported when they leave prison. Housing is an essential part of the desistance process.

Keywords Housing · Halfway house · Release from prison · Safe and supported housing

INTRODUCTION

One of the challenges when discussing housing for former prisoners is that much of the literature focuses on paroled prisoners. Prisoners can be released from prison in a number of ways, through parole, a temporary absence, on a statutory release, or at the end of their sentence. While examining paroled individuals' housing issues is important, it ignores housing challenges for those released from prison without parole support. Researchers have yet to study provincial prisoners who are more likely to leave prison without parole support and thus have increased housing challenges.

© The Author(s), under exclusive license to Springer Nature
Switzerland AG 2024
A. Sheppard, *Life on The Outside*,
https://doi.org/10.1007/978-3-031-63817-6_3

Further, women, in particular, often have limited housing options when released from prison. Men are more likely to return from prison to wives/girlfriends/mothers who have managed their home life in their absence (Balis, 2007). However, if a woman lived in an apartment before her incarceration, she might lose her housing if she cannot pay rent while in prison. Other women may not want to return to living in unsafe and abusive environments (Maidment, 2006).

The lack of safe housing is a significant barrier for women leaving prison in NL, resulting in some women remaining in prison after being granted parole or a temporary absence. There is no dedicated halfway house for women in NL, impacting women in the provincial prison. Provincial prison staff can grant temporary absences for those who have served two-thirds of their sentence. However, without a dedicated halfway house for women, many women are not granted temporary absences, meaning that they have to remain in prison while eligible for release.

While there are no dedicated halfway houses for women released from prisons in NL, there are some options. Westbridge House, operated by the John Howard Society of Newfoundland and Labrador, is a co-ed facility for "adult offenders on day parole, full parole, statutory release, a temporary release, or a probation order" (John Howard Society of Newfoundland & Labrador, 2023). Westbridge House is located on the west coast of the island of Newfoundland. Throughout my work at NLCCW, a few women from that area of the province have accessed Westbridge House on parole or a temporary release. Other women have stated that they would rather stay in prison than go to Westbridge House due to lack of services, isolation from supports, and male residents.

Another option for women leaving prison on parole or a temporary absence is Emmanuel House, a treatment centre under Stella's Circle's umbrella. Emmanuel House offers a therapeutic environment where men and women over 18 can live while addressing their social and emotional challenges (Stella's Circle, 2024). CSC contracts Emmanuel House to provide two beds for parolees. There is also an arrangement with the Government of Newfoundland and Labrador to provide beds for release from provincial prisons. There is often a significant waitlist, limiting women's ability to access the option when leaving prison. Furthermore, given that Emmanuel House is a treatment centre, not all women qualify to attend. As well some women may also not be interested in attending an intensive treatment programme on release from prison. Moreover, both options are co-ed facilities, which may be problematic for women who would not want to live with men (Maidment, 2006).

Women I interviewed stated that housing was key to supporting their release from prison and navigating longer-term desistance. The Housing First approach asserts that housing is a fundamental human right; everyone is entitled to housing. Ideally, communities should provide homeless individuals with permanent housing as quickly as possible while providing services to maintain their housing. The basic assumption here is that people need housing first before working on other issues, such as addiction or criminality (Gaetz et al., 2013). While the women I interviewed did not name the Housing First philosophy, they certainly understood it. They identified housing as the first step needed after prison and acknowledged how desistance is near impossible without safe housing.

In this chapter, I examine what women and service providers say about housing, including challenges in finding appropriate housing and the need for supported housing. I first share the various housing arrangements women I interviewed found after release. I then explore how these arrangements impact desistance processes.

CHALLENGES IN HOUSING

Women in the current study used a variety of housing options when released from prison. Eight of the sixteen women interviewed went to Emmanuel House, a pseudo-halfway house, on release as a parole condition or temporary absence. They all were able to secure housing after completing parole or temporary absence with Stella's Circle staff's help. The other eight women in my sample had a variety of housing arrangements on release. Some women were able to keep their housing while incarcerated for several reasons, including short incarcerations (two women), negotiations with a landlord (one woman), or having a family member pay the rent (one woman). One woman stayed with friends on release, another with her ex-boyfriend, and another was released on a temporary absence with arrangements supported by Stella's Circle Housing (an unstaffed but supported apartment). Finally, one woman was released to a homeless shelter but referred to a case management programme with Stella's Circle, where she found permanent housing about a month after her release. At the time of this writing, all women but one has not returned to prison. Given these successes in desistance, it is not a coincidence that the majority of women interviewed had some kind of housing arrangement on release.

However, the diversity of housing arrangements for women on release from prison illustrates a lack of adequate housing support. What exists in NL are ad hoc arrangements for women. Some women can access formal supports through Stella's Circle, and some women rely on their survival skills to have their housing needs met. As Robyn stated, for some women, "you go back to exactly where you were before you went in." In her words, Robyn illustrates the importance of having safe, reliable housing on release from prison. She asks how society expects women to change when they are back in the same situation as before their incarceration.

On the other hand, the women who were able to access Emmanuel House stated that they benefitted from "landing" somewhere staffed, safe, and in a sober environment after prison. As Mary stated, "Emmanuel House saved my life." Mary said she felt safe and was able to address her anxiety and depression, which allowed her, when she went home, to move on with her life in a positive way.

While Emmanuel House was a helpful place to stay when initially released from prison, many women expressed concerns about finding adequate housing. For example, Beth, who had stayed at Emmanuel House, stated she would return to live with her family after her temporary absence. Staying with her family was not what she wanted, but she explained that a housing shortage exists in her home community:

Beth: Right now, I'm just struggling going back home cuz, and I'm still living with my mom, and I'm (age redacted) years old, and I still don't have a place of my own. I'm just struggling about that. I have a hard time thinking about it, like going through this situation when you're (age redacted) years old, and you're grown-up. Yeah, as a woman, and you don't have a place of your own.

Amy: It feels like you're a kid?

Beth: Yeah, living with my mom, my dad.

Amy: What's the situation like in (location redacted) for housing? Is it easy to get your own place?

Beth: No, no, it's not easy.

Amy: What's the situation? Do you have to apply for housing?

Beth: Yeah, I applied for housing like three years ago, four years ago, but no, that was five years ago because I wanted to have my own place because I never have space.

My conversation with Beth highlights challenges in finding adequate housing in rural and Northern areas of the province. Her words show she values having her own housing, which she considers a step towards independence and being a "grown-up." For Beth, her independence is a crucial component in her future goals, including education, employment, and living a sober, crime-free life.

Beyond the general lack of housing to support women post-release from custody is the lack of *safe* housing. Gloria explains her challenges in accessing safe housing and finding a drug-free environment. She references the day the court granted her release, noting, "… I walked into my friend's place, and there was (drug) paraphernalia everywhere. I'm like, oh, what am I gonna do? So I called (another friend). I'm like, can I please stay with you? So that's what I did, and I went and stayed with her." Gloria had been remanded for two and a half months and was released on house arrest. Gloria arranged her own housing situation to stay with a friend, explaining that release planning while on remand is difficult because there is an unknown release date. Gloria's quote highlights issues with addiction and challenges associated with housing and the commitment to desistance. Gloria decided to leave her housing arrangement when she saw drug paraphernalia. Leaving her housing arrangement was not an easy choice. Because she was on house arrest, Gloria had to report her living arrangement to her probation officer and ask that another housing arrangement be approved. Disclosure to her probation officer means potentially divulging the reason for the move (drug paraphernalia), which can mean extra scrutiny for Gloria by authorities. Gloria was very committed to her recovery from drugs and believed that she needed to move, despite moving not being an easy process. Many women in the current study will return to places and people where criminal/drug lifestyles are the norm.

SERVICES PROVIDERS: SUPPORTED HOUSING

Service providers identified housing as a critical component of supporting women in desistance and a pro-social lifestyle. However, service providers stated that women do not just need a house but need supported housing, including wrap-around services to help with social and life skills, mental health, and substance use issues. Supportive housing, broadly defined, is independent housing linked to service providers who can provide mental health services and concrete supports that foster eviction prevention (Rog, 2004).

Pearl, a service provider, acknowledges that the ad hoc arrangements for women after being released mean that women may end up in unsupported or even dangerous situations because they need somewhere to live. She states:

> Sometimes, if it comes down to like, they just need a roof over their head. That can be kind of a challenge, right, and on where their family is. Sometimes they're kind of at the mercy of whatever their familial support is because that's kind of where they can get housed. So it would be great to see a halfway house in St. John's for women or some kind of supportive housing.

Pearl recognized the need for a house and that women may not have sound natural supports systems. She suggests that supported housing is needed whereby women can access services to support their pro-social goals. All service providers stated that housing was a significant barrier for women. While most interviewed women were released from prison into some sort of housing arrangement, most were released to a halfway house. From there, halfway house staff helped women find housing in the community. Service providers have worked with a diverse group of women over many years and strongly advocate that housing remains a fundamental barrier for women leaving prison.

CONCLUSION

Given these diverse experiences with housing on release from prison, housing plays an integral part for women planning to change their lifestyles. Most women in this study had access to housing on release from prison, which they felt supported their ability to desist. However, there is a shortage of housing options for women leaving prison. For some women, a safe option is not readily available. On the other hand, for women who were released to Emmanuel House, having a safe, drug-free, and staffed housing option was critical in making a plan for future desistance and future housing.

REFERENCES

Balis, A. (2007). Female prisoners and the case for gender-specific treatment and reentry programs. In R. Greifinger (Ed.), *Public health behind bars* (pp. 320–332). Springer.

Gaetz, S., Scott, F., & Gulliver, T. (2013). *Housing first in Canada: Supporting communities to end homelessness.* Canadian Homelessness Research Network Press. Retrieved February 29, 2024, from https://www.homelesshub.ca/sites/default/files/HousingFirstInCanada.pdf

John Howard Society of Newfoundland and Labrador. (2023). *Westbridge House.* Retrieved February 29, 2024, from https://www.johnhowardnl.ca/services/residential/west-bridge-house/

Maidment, M. R. (2006). *Doing time on the outside: Deconstructing the benevolent community.* University of Toronto Press.

Rog, D. (2004). The evidence on supported housing. *Psychiatric Rehabilitation Journal, 27*(4), 334–344.

Stella's Circle. (2024). Retrieved February 29, 2024, from https://stellascircle.ca/

CHAPTER 4

Service Delivery: Who Can Help?

Abstract Criminalized women often have high needs and require support while incarcerated and on release. In this chapter, women and service providers discuss what is needed to enhance existing supports and what services must be added to ensure that formerly incarcerated women get what they need. Formerly incarcerated women stated that they need more of existing services but that these services can be improved with added frequency and attention to gender and trauma. Service providers advise that there are multiple barriers for women on release from prison and suggest ways of making services more accessible. Women interviewed took personal responsibility for changes needed for the desistance process, while service providers saw the multiple barriers impeding their process. I argue that both these ideas are needed to support desistance processes. Women need to access services, but service providers must support their agency while advocating to minimize barriers.

Keywords Services · Gender-responsive · Trauma-informed · Prison · Community-based · Barriers

© The Author(s), under exclusive license to Springer Nature Switzerland AG 2024
A. Sheppard, *Life on The Outside*,
https://doi.org/10.1007/978-3-031-63817-6_4

INTRODUCTION

Women in prison have high levels of needs and vulnerabilities (Bateman & Hazel, 2014). The challenges women face on reentry are compounded by existing gendered inequalities (Maidment, 2006). Thus, reentry considerations must be gender-responsive and trauma-informed and help women find a sense of "agency" (Balis, 2007). Gendered inequalities mean that women returning from prison are often returning to the same conditions that they left: poverty, unemployment, challenging (often abusive) family dynamics, as well as mental health and substance use issues. Formerly incarcerated women may have a social capital deficit, referring to women's lack of access to social networks that traditionally provide pro-social capital, such as employment, before and after prison. Being tied to negative support networks hinders women's reintegration into the community (Cobbina, 2010). Women return home with the same lack of resources but now bring their prison record, which further thwarts efforts to find employment (Balis, 2007).

Societies should share an interest in preparing prisoners for successful reentry into the community; after all, most prisoners will leave prison and return to communities (Sieter & Kadela, 2003; Travis, 2005). Reentry support includes supporting women as they continuously and actively choose to desist from crime.

Women I interviewed expressed that they navigate desistance by using services offered both in prison and in the community. Most women stated that quality services exist in the community and prison. However, they expressed concerns (i) about the availability of services (e.g., more were needed), (ii) the frequency of service provision (more often was desired), and (iii) with how services are delivered, suggesting that services must be gender and trauma-responsive. These concerns are discussed in this chapter.

MORE SERVICES NEEDED

Women interviewed acknowledge that existing services at NLCCW, with one exception (the psychiatrist), are helpful but provided too infrequently. For example, the women interviewed stated that the psychologist[1] in the NLCCW is helpful. However, he has limited time to see the women in the institution, leaving women to see him biweekly or less frequently. Robyn states:

> I think that counselling needs to be available more often. (The psychologist) is an awesome counsellor, like amazing. His job is probably one of the best things about that place in total, but like you see him once a week, maybe. Yeah, maybe every two weeks. Yeah, you know and like you don't know when you're going to see him either so you can't like, you know what I mean? It's like you're sitting there and have no idea when you'll get your chance, right, and then there's times that you were supposed to, and it's just not reliable. It's not consistent, right, there's no consistency to it at all like structure, reliability like sometimes you're told you're going to go see him and there's something comes up, and now you can't see him. Like if something happens or like yeah, some random emergency or a guard can't come in, so we were all locked down. It's just...there's no consistency to it.

Women were largely positive about the services provided and the staff at the prison. However, they wanted access to services more frequently and throughout the days, evenings, nights, and weekends. Robyn's comments above are typical of other women interviewed who identified that the psychologist is empathetic; he listens and helps women develop plans for their lives outside of prison.

Robyn also identifies the lack of consistency in services offered. She states that during emergencies or when there are staffing shortages, they are "locked down." This means that prisoners remain in the cells for the duration of the emergency or staffing shortage. Security concerns are cited as the reason for these lockdowns, as there are inadequate staff

---

[1] The psychologist who provided services to women at NLCCW at the time that women in this study were interviewed is no longer working at NLCCW, much to the disappointment of many women. The provincial health authority has since taken over the majority of mental health services at NLCCW, as recommended by the Jesso report (2018). Stella's Circle continues to provide services through a contract with the Department of Justice and Public Safety.

to respond to prisoners while they are in common areas. Lockdowns can impede services, such as groups and schooling. However, individual counselling services can go ahead as scheduled.

Women interviewed acknowledged that Stella's Circle services, which are offered in prison, helped encourage them to think about their needs, such as substance misuse or problematic patterns of behaviour. Women also stated that they felt that Stella's Circle was non-judgemental and treated women with respect. For example, in a discussion about her goals, Laura shared that Stella's Circle staff was supportive in helping her choose a "better life," which, for her, means a drug-free life. She states, "It's nice to have people to give you that confidence that you don't really have all the time." Similarly, Judy, a formerly incarcerated woman, shared that Stella's Circle staff validated women in prison by helping them to see their self-worth. She states, "They didn't have any self-worth. And you guys gave them that. No matter what you have done, no matter what your background you're a human being, you're loved." Judy believes that Stella's Circle staff treated incarcerated women with the respect that they often did not feel, allowing them to internalize feelings of self-worth.

Furthermore, Ali stated that Stella's Circle was vital in helping her understand her path to recovery from addiction. I asked Ali what was helpful when she was released. She explained that programmes through Stella's Circle helped her identify natural supports such as family and friends and helped her identify harmful patterns in her social life. Ali shares:

Ali: I've learned a lot in these programs (Stella's Circle) and stuff. Because I didn't get Facebook back or nothing. So, I got no friends. I got one decent, one good friend that I've been best friends with since we were five, but she lives up in Ontario, just had a little boy last year and everything.

Amy: When you say that you didn't get Facebook back, that was your choice or was it a condition?

Ali: No, that was my choice. Yeah. I got no social media at all. I sit down on my phone and play solitaire.

Amy: Why is that a good thing?

Ali: It's just trouble. I know too many, too many people that are not good people to know in the city. Yeah, and I know the majority of them.

For Ali, through attending programming with Stella's Circle, she learned that disconnecting from Facebook and, therefore, disconnecting from "not good people to know" will help meet her goals of living a pro-social life.

Many interviewed women identified ad hoc services such as equine therapy, horticultural therapy, occupational training, the dog programme, bible study, and even doing chores in prison as giving them a sense of hope and purpose. When asked about services, Mary stated, "Like I did all the courses that were offered, and they needed someone in the wintertime to help shovel and look after the dogs. And that was the big thing. I love the dogs." Ali also shared that "the spirit horse thing that they did at NLCCW that was really cool." These services, such as equine therapy (Spirit Horse) and the dog programme, are ad hoc services that are offered when resources are available. While they are not consistent, they impact women who can participate. Again, these are examples of women wanting more of the good services that are provided.

Interviewees also acknowledged many of the staff, including Correctional Officers and Classification Officers, in NLCCW as helpful in that they listened to women when they needed to talk. While not all staff have an empathic ear or are available to talk, interviewed women shared that some prison staff were helpful during their time in prison. Women noted that staff needed more training to deal with the number of mental health issues presented by incarcerated women. As Mary states, "The guards were excellent. You know, everyone was good to me." However, Mary also acknowledged that while the guards were friendly and would talk to women who were having a mental health crisis or just going through a difficult time, they were not trained to handle mental health crises adequately. Mary stated: "I've seen the young ones (inmates) in there that they really needed help, and they were never given the help, and the guards couldn't do anything. I mean, yes, they could talk to them. I don't think the doctor did anything." Mary's frustrations are seeing other women suffering mental health crises while imprisoned and feeling that staff were inadequately equipped to support women. Further, she felt that the medical services (psychiatry) did nothing to help.

While the women interviewed identified existing services as helpful, empathetic, and non-judgemental, the consistent complaint remained about the infrequent service provision. Many women interviewed stated that services needed to be available when they and other women they served time with were experiencing a crisis in prison. Services such as the psychologist and Stella's Circle are in prison for a limited number of hours and provide a specific service: individual and group counselling, not crisis management. Women, like Mary above, acknowledged that, for the most part, correctional officers are empathetic and are willing to talk; however, they are not trained adequately in mental health, thus limited in their ability to help women navigate mental health crises. When women experienced a mental health crisis, they felt that their needs were not met. These feelings are in line with Jesso's (2018) report, which followed an investigation into four deaths by suicide in NL's prison system within a short period. She concluded that there are inadequate responses to mental health crises in the prison system.

Women identified boredom as a significant issue in prison and a challenge for their mental health. Women identified the need for outdoor recreation as a requirement for mental health. Monica shared: "I think personally for myself, where I have bad anxiety if you gotta go out to the yard to be able to get some air and you should be able to get air. And I don't think that's right (that we can't go out)." Furthermore, they felt that additional services, such as therapeutic groups and spiritual activities, organized recreation such as arts and crafts or physical activities, and social activities (e.g., friendly visitors, volunteering) are needed. There is inadequate space and staffing, challenging the prison's ability to provide increased services. However, as Robyn states:

They just need more groups in general. There should be like at least one thing every day. Because you spend so much time in there, and then when you get out, I was like, well, I just had all this time sitting around doing nothing. I could've used that towards it (planning for release), right, but you can't do much there because, like, who are you going to talk to? How can you get anything on the go for yourself when you're on the outside? Because you can't use the internet. You can't call to look through your options and stuff.

Robyn implies she has time she could spend making plans for the future. However, she asserts that prison time is a waste without someone to help with those plans. Ward and Maruna (2007) argue that the key to successful "rehabilitation" is for service providers to listen to the prisoners. They state that prisoners have told them: "No one else can rehabilitate you. You rehabilitate yourself" (Ward & Maruna, 2007, p. 16). Having a sense of agency or belief that one can exert influence on oneself and the environment promotes desistance (Maruna, 2001). Indeed, Robyn's ideas assert that she has the agency needed but lack of services means that she cannot exercise the agency needed to make plans for desistance.

Women in the study maintained an agentic view of change, meaning that they saw themselves as responsible for making the changes needed to move away from criminal lifestyles and towards a new, pro-social life. When I asked formerly incarcerated women how service providers could help with pro-social change, all women stated, "You have to want it." They further stated that service providers could not do anything to help without the initial desire from the individual. This idea fits with Maruna's (2001) idea of desisters needing an optimistic view of their ability to control their own destiny. In essence, women believe they are the agents of their own desistance process; desistance is not something that just happens; *you* have to make it happen. Despite the multiple barriers identified by both formerly incarcerated women and service providers, women believe that they have the power to make changes in their lives. Most women in the current study were able to do so.

Reflecting on Robyn's words reveals a need for services and programmes to be responsive to the criminalized person's needs. According to Robyn, programme design should include the interests, abilities, and aspirations of those incarcerated. Furthermore, prisoners should help direct practitioners develop intervention plans that assist incarcerated persons with acquiring skills and accessing the relevant internal and external resources to achieve personally meaningful goals (Fortune et al., 2012; Maruna, 2001; Ward, 2002). Women want service providers' objectives to include helping them look at their lives through a new lens and determine future goals. Instead of programming that aims to "fix" people, person-focused interventions should be used by providing them with skills to change how they "think, feel, act" (Fortune et al., 2012, p. 649). Given adequate resources, service providers can begin person-based interventions during incarceration.

Person-centred care is rooted in a healthcare model that aligns healthcare services and settings with an individual's unique needs. To achieve person-centred care, an individual must have access to the right services in the right setting (World Health Organization, 2013). The model can be extended to working with incarcerated prisoners and on release. Pearson and colleagues (2015) suggest that in a person-centred model of service delivery for prisoners:

Practitioners would work with individual offenders for a time-limited 'pathway' based on identification prior to release, support 'through the prison gate,' and support in the community. We envisaged that the intervention would be judiciously modifiable to local contexts; link to, and support, coordination of existing resources (rather than being a standalone, all-encompassing service); and provide some form of ongoing care and support.

They put forth a model that begins in prison before release and provides wrap-around support when released into the community. For services to prisoners to be genuinely person-centred, practitioners must recognize the person within the prisoner. The Good Lives Model is a strength-based model that advocates that practitioners help prisoners examine their own goals, abilities, and interests to achieve pro-social behaviours and eventual desistance (Fortune et al., 2012). Within the Good Lives Model, the practitioner works to help the prisoner identify how they envision a good life and how the individual can achieve that good life.

Truly person-centred interventions for prisoners must include both a deep understanding of the individual's goals and an understanding of systems that impact achieving these goals. As stated in the WHO's (2013) definition of person-centred health care, the right services must be in place in the right places. Having services in the right place at the right time is a challenge when working with prisoners and those on release. Often, adequate services are not in place to help a former prisoner achieve their goals, no matter how realistic or modest these goals may be. Thus, person-centred care for prisoners also involves advocacy with an understanding of the barriers faced by former prisoners.

Gender-responsive and Trauma-informed

Women stated community-based services were not always attuned to the women's needs. Specifically, services offered are neither gender-responsive nor trauma-informed. Within the criminal justice system, gender-responsive services acknowledge that gender makes a difference in how a person experiences that system and the wider world (Covington & Bloom, 2007). Gender-responsive services recognize that women enter into the criminal justice system on different pathways than men. Women experience the criminalization process, prison, and supervision differently and experience differences in substance abuse, trauma histories, relationships, and responsibilities (Balis, 2007; Efleet, 2021; Rutter & Barr, 2021). Given these differences, services provided to women must create an environment based on safety and address specific needs, such as relationships with children and other family members.

If services for criminalized women are to be gender-responsive, it follows that services must understand the impacts of trauma. The impacts of trauma are far-reaching and are often intertwined with substance misuse. Trauma impacts physical health, mental health, employment, and educational opportunities (Covington & Bloom, 2007; Crowder, 2016; Matheson et al., 2015). Within trauma-informed services, the goal is establishing safety and interventions based on improving coping skills (Matheson et al., 2015).

While interviewees did not use the terms gender-responsive or trauma-informed, their experiences revealed the service gaps in said areas. For example, Katie relayed a story about needing to go to a local non-profit that provides a host of services to vulnerable and marginalized populations, including food, clothes, and medical services. She stated, ".... I have to go up there (a local non-profit), and I'm frightened to death. I should have been three weeks ago. Yeah, but I'm going. Yeah, I just got to make myself some go. Yes. I'm afraid of who (former male associates) I'm going to see up there." Likewise, Laura states, "I don't go to the (local non-profit). Not for anything. There is too much drug trade, and up there whacked out of their heads and getting into fights. It's just not a good scene." Both Katie and Laura cite violence and the drug trade as reasons they are afraid to access an otherwise helpful service.

As Katie, Laura, and others explained, the non-profit provides essential services, but many women avoid the non-profit agency because men, too, access services there. Women state that it is a small city, and they easily run into people they know, including ex-partners or drug dealers. Women fear running into men they know, particularly men with more violent reputations who frequent the non-profit. Katie's example illustrates the challenges of providing gender-responsive services in an agency that serves a large, heterogeneous population. Katie is afraid to see men from her past who are associated with drug use and crime. Laura fears violent men. For many women, their pathways to crime are associated with relationships with men (O'Brien, 2001; Rutter & Barr, 2021). Thus, services must recognize the unique needs of criminalized women to provide them with adequate services.

Another example of how services are not gender-responsive or trauma-informed is the co-ed parole options for women. Through my work at NLCCW, I know that a few women from the province's west coast have accessed Westbridge House on parole or temporary release. In my field journal, I noted that when given the option of being paroled to Westbridge House, some women would rather stay in prison than attend Westbridge House due to the lack of services, isolation from support, and the house's male residents. Furthermore, the other option for women on parole, Emmanuel House, is also co-ed. Women interviewed in this study spoke about discomfort with men in spaces meant to provide them with a sense of safety, such as the co-ed options for release. Their discomfort is likely rooted in their experiences of trauma. Experiences of trauma are gendered, and women are more likely to experience trauma at the hands of an intimate male partner or other family members (O'Brien, 2001). These traumatic experiences are compounded by the nature of intimate relationships, adding a sense of betrayal and confusion (Covington, 2008). Therefore, the presence of men in what should be considered safe spaces can be challenging. I am not suggesting that women avoid men and co-ed spaces, but service providers need to recognize the challenges associated with male presence for women. Furthermore, we need to consider creating women-only spaces as an option.

Concerns about men's presence in service-oriented spaces are an example that speaks to the need for services offered to be trauma-informed. A substantial number, 33%, of women imprisoned in Canada's federal prisons are diagnosed with Post-Traumatic Stress Disorder (Derken et al., 2017). While significant, many more women report histories of sexual (68%) and physical abuse (86%) than have been diagnosed with Post-Traumatic Stress Disorder (Zinger, 2014). Thus, many more women may be suffering due to trauma histories than are formally diagnosed with a mental illness. Researchers and practitioners characterize trauma-informed care as requiring a paradigm shift that requires social service workers to acknowledge the impact that trauma, violence, and abuse can have on people's lives and development (Evans & Coccoma, 2014). Trauma-informed practitioners understand that regaining control over their environment is a priority when someone has been traumatized. Therefore, there is an emphasis on safety, choice, trustworthiness, collaboration, and empowerment (Blanch et al., 2012). Given the experiences of trauma that incarcerated women have had, these factors are essential when considering how to deliver services.

Women's concerns about women-only and trauma-informed spaces are in line with literature that states programming and services provided for women involved in the criminal justice system, both in and out of prison, must be gender-responsive (Balis, 2007; Covington, 2008; Covington & Bloom, 2007; Kilty, 2012; Matheson et al., 2015). Gender-responsive services are effective in meeting treatment needs for women. Clinical services for addiction treatment that focus on women's specific issues and needs are more effective for women than traditional programmes initially designed for men (Grella, 1999). Therefore, services must keep within the unique needs of women in spaces and services traditionally thought of as male-dominated spaces, such as prison, homelessness, or addiction.

Formerly incarcerated women were clear on what they believed would help them during the process of being released from prison: practical support, such as housing and services designed with them in mind to address their unique needs. Women expressed a need to be "set up" when leaving prison—having immediate needs addressed before release so they can go about the business of a lifestyle change. Women wanted to change and stated that change happens first within themselves. Although there are many services in place that can help the change, ultimately, as they state, "you have to want it."

Increased Mental Health and Addiction Services

Service providers stated that more mental health and addiction services are needed to adequately address the needs of criminalized women in the community and prison. When I asked service providers if there are sufficient mental health and addiction services, they all stated that there are not enough services, citing wait times and lack of funding as problems. For example, Grace stated that there are year-long waits for psychiatry referrals. Furthermore, she stated that out-of-province treatment might be an option for some women. However, funding is difficult to arrange as funding requires advocacy from a psychiatrist to the Department of Health and Community Services. Likewise, service providers stated that there are inadequate services available in prison. Faye suggested that prison services must be available "on-site and 24/7," meaning that a mental health service provider should be in prison at all times to respond to the needs of women.

Service providers were able to name many services offered by government-run health authorities. However, many service providers believed these services could not meet the needs of criminalized women. Sue, a service provider, stated that the services are available, but the women she works with believe these services are not useful. Sue explained that women had not experienced mental health services at the hospital as helpful; "It is not one size fits all." Sue implies here that the mental health services offered at the hospital do not account for individual needs but rather provide a blanket service in an effort to address everyone's needs. Similarly, Nina indicated that her client feedback makes it challenging to decide where to refer clients, stating.

> I find it hard to think of where to (refer) when people talk about wanting to go to, you know, rehab or detox. I hear it's not great, and I don't have something that I feel like is up my sleeve where I can be like, here you go, here's a great solution.

Service providers felt that, while there are services that provide mental health and addiction support, these services do not meet the unique needs of criminalized women, particularly those who have complex mental health and addiction issues.

Throughout interviews with service providers, I experienced a sense that criminalized women are an extra difficult population to serve. Service providers asserted that there are inadequate services in place to address the needs of criminalized women. While formerly incarcerated women interviewed stated that the quality of services is good, just not enough of the services. The difference in service providers' versus women's responses may be explained by whom I interviewed versus who service providers refer to when responding to interview questions. I interviewed women who were actively engaged in desisting. Service providers are working with women who may be still in active addiction, crime, etc., thus providing contrasting perspectives—they are perhaps speaking about women who do not feel they are engaged in the process of change.

Fewer Barriers

Interviewed service providers identified several barriers for women trying to access services in the community. These barriers include having to make appointments, waitlists, and the requirement to be abstinent from drug use.

Many services in the community require a referral or the ability to make and show up for appointments. Services providers stated that these requirements could be a challenge for some criminalized women, particularly those who are street-entrenched or homeless. For some women, making a phone call or needing a referral can be a barrier. As service providers stated, the more hoops people have to jump through, the more challenging they find accessing services. For example, some women may not have a phone, or service providers may not be immediately available when they have access to a phone, such as a friend's or community service. As Pearl states:

> I think the barriers specific to making phone calls or needing a referral or like the specifics that women have to undergo. Be it maybe paperwork, be it forms, be it a referral, be it like a phone call. Whatever those little barriers are. They are hurdles that they have to get over to access those services or get that first point of contact. I think they are hugely overwhelming for women, especially when they're in transition or their couch surfing, or they're like working a job, or they're trying to they're running all over the place, and you don't have a phone.

Pearl acknowledges that the challenge for women is arriving at that first point of contact with service providers. Compounding the problem of making the first contact is frustration with waitlists for services. Grace says, "I have a 26-person waitlist, with probably 8 to 12 months wait time. Psychiatry only takes referrals from GPs (general practitioners), and they have a two-year waitlist." Waitlists and difficulty making the first contact evidence the need for various services available to women at differing levels of ability, motivation, and need. Meeting women where they are, both literally and figuratively, is a critical component in working with the population. Street-based work is essential in working with women who are homeless or street-entrenched.

Services provided by those interviewed represented a mix of approaches to working with women, fitting with the diversity of criminalized women's needs. Services included drop-in, case management, street-based outreach, counselling (both drop-in and by appointment), prison in-reach, therapeutic group work, social/recreational activities, employment support, and housing support. Providing a wide variety of services means that the diversity of women's needs can be better met.

Some services offered by interview participants are provided exclusively to criminalized women, while other services are offered to women only or the public. Some women have expressed the need to have space for criminalized women only—a safe space to acknowledge experiences with court or prison and not fear stigma or judgement from others. For example, formerly incarcerated women expressed the need for services with other women who have been to prison. Nevertheless, service providers also noted that some women did not want to be referred to the Just Us Women's Centre (a programme within Stella's Circle) because it is for criminalized women only. Some women did not want to encounter women with criminal histories as there was a fear of falling back into the lifestyle.

Faye says, "So one of the things is that Stella's Circle is one of the main referral sources, but for some of the women, they don't want to come here because they don't want to see certain people that they have been inside with, they don't want to be faced with the temptation." The idea presented here, that some women do not want to associate with women they knew from prison, fits with theories of desistance that propose "knifing off" one's past contributes to desistance. Maruna and Roy (2007) suggest that "knifing off" the past may be a part of early desistance when it is essential to distance from people who may influence a return to old behaviours. However, they further suggest that as the desistance process continues, cognitive shifts that move away from criminal thinking are required to desist in the long term. I put forth that desistance as a process has implications for programming for criminalized women, whereby programme delivery must recognize the stages where women are and then support desistance within that context. For example, supporting "knifing off" a past associated with criminal associates may encourage women to access services with a "mixed group" of women attending.

Another issue key for service providers to understand when working with women in the criminal justice system is substance use/misuse and addiction. Service providers identified barriers such as requiring abstinence from substance use to access programming. Vivian explains:

If there's times when there's addictions issues involved, they (criminalized women) become even more disengaged. Not just because of the lifestyle stuff, but also I think their experiences with professionals have often been that professionals don't want them around if they're under the influence.

Some programmes require abstinence, like in-patient treatment. However, other community-based services require refraining from substance use to attend appointments or groups. However, service providers may be flexible to meet for some services while an individual is under the influence of a substance,

Many community-based agencies are taking a harm-reduction approach that suggests abstinence from substances not be a requirement to access services. However, Vivian's quote suggests that many clients have taken the message about abstinence to heart and feel they cannot access services if they are using drugs or alcohol. Therefore, messaging must be clear and outright, stating that active substance use is not a barrier to accessing particular services.

CONCLUSION

Women see their situation and, arguably, through their incarceration, which exposes them to neo-liberal ideas of responsibilization, hold themselves responsible for their lives. For example, the women interviewed suggested that the individual has to reach out and seek support. Over and over, women stated, "You have to want it." Women focused on the changes that they needed to make. All women interviewed stated that they wanted their lives to be different when they left prison.

Formerly incarcerated women interviewed all took personal responsibility for the changes they needed to make. Women's assertion that the individual must be invested in desistance fits with Maruna's (2001), who suggested that for a criminalized individual to "go straight," they must generate a gradual shift in self-narrative. He states that the narrative of desisters differs from those active in a criminal lifestyle in three fundamental ways: (1) the establishment of core beliefs that characterize "true self," (2) an optimistic view of control over destiny, and (3) a desire to be productive and give back to society. Maruna (2001) suggests that those who can "rehabilitate" generate a positive self-narrative, stating that they are still good people even though they have done wrong. Furthermore, Maruna (2001) states that successful desisters can reach back to find the "old me" to find positive roles and sense themselves as intelligent and better than a common criminal. Thus, Maruna (2001) argues that desistance is not merely something that happens to a person but is an active process. Maruna's vision of desistance is an important one for service providers to understand as they support women's desistance. Service providers can help promote a positive self-narrative. For some women, starting to create a self-narrative is nuanced and new, yet for others, the narrative has become a more entrenched part of their identity.

While I cannot say if all women in my study will successfully desist from crime (at the time of this writing, one woman has returned to prison), interviewees are engaged in the process of developing a self-narrative that involves change talk moving towards desistance. Furthermore, to help women achieve their goals, service providers need to work with criminalized women to explain systemic issues and how issues impact women's circumstances and ability to desist from crime. Thereby, women can understand that "failure" to desist from crime is not necessarily a personal failure but a failure of systems to provide adequate care and support.

The idea of balancing these two views, personal responsibility and systems' failure, is vital to reveal what formerly incarcerated women need to do to change their circumstances. For example, when interviewing service providers, I asked questions about criminalized women's desistance. For example, asking women what they identified as goals for change after release. Some service providers interpreted questions about women's role in desistance as judgemental of criminalized women. Service providers did not answer the question but pivoted to what community and government agencies needed to help criminalize women. As I went about my interviews with service providers, I adjusted the questions, acknowledging that they may seem judgemental. However, I was still interested in the role that women felt that they played in their desistance journeys.

Criminalized women, conversely, were not bothered by the questions and freely answered, suggesting diverse changes they needed to live a different, crime-free life. Criminalized women asserted their agency to act in particular ways related to crime-free lifestyles, while service providers focused on the contexts of such choices. I have combined both voices, providing a nuanced view of criminalized women's lives, which values both their assertions of agency and the context of their agency.

I also question service providers' (and I include myself) resistance to women's positions of taking responsibility. There are systemic barriers, and it is my job, both as a researcher and as a service provider, to identify and mitigate barriers. However, I also need to listen to women telling me they have a role. Dismissing women's concerns as "buying into neoliberal rhetoric" that insists on personal responsibility and asserting that all problems are systemic denies women the agency they need to dictate their lives. The combination of issues at play here must be acknowledged. Desistance literature emphasizes personal responsibility, but there needs to be an acknowledgement that personal responsibility does not happen in a vacuum. Implications for service providers are to work with women's ideas of personal responsibility while educating them that systemic issues will impact their journey towards that "better life."

Barr's (2019) Social Harms approach to desistance may be a helpful framework for an academic understanding of some aspects of women's desistance in the current project. However, evidence from my interviews with service providers suggests that they are already working from a social harms approach in their daily work with criminalized women and other marginalized groups. Service providers identified social harms, such as poverty, lack of community connections, racism, and sexism, as barriers to women's health, well-being, and safety. Service providers are less concerned with the process of desistance as a concept and are more concerned with helping people move away from harm and meet their goals, which may include desistance from crime. Women themselves identified some of these issues and the harmful impacts of addiction on their criminal lifestyle. Thus, I see Barr's (2019) social harms approach supporting how service providers in the current study have already been working with criminalized women, helping them move from social harms by working with individuals and systemic advocacy.

REFERENCES

Balis, A. (2007). Female prisoners and the case for gender-specific treatment and reentry programs. In R. Greifinger (Ed.), *Public health behind bars* (pp. 320–332). Springer.

Barr, Ú. (2019). *Desisting sisters*. Springer.

Bateman, T., & Hazel, N. (2014). *Resettlement of girls and young women: Research summary*. University of Salford.

Blanch, A., Filson, B., Penney, D., & Cave, C. (2012). *Engaging women in trauma-informed peer support: A guidebook*. National Center for Trauma-Informed Care. Retrieved March 2, 2024, from https://www.theannainstitute.org/Andrea%20Blanch%20TIWA/EngagingWomeninTIPeerSupportGuidebook.pdf

Cobbina, J. E. (2010). Reintegration success and failure: Factors impacting reintegration among incarcerated and formerly incarcerated women. *Journal of Offender Rehabilitation, 49*(3), 210–232.

Covington, S. (2008). Women and addiction: A trauma-informed approach. *Journal of Psychoactive Drugs, 40*(5), 377–385.

Covington, S., & Bloom, B. (2007). Gender-responsive treatment and services in correctional settings. *Women & Therapy, 29*(3/4), 9–33.

Crowder, R. (2016). Mindfulness based feminist therapy: The intermingling edges of self-compassion and social justice. *Journal of Religion & Spirituality in Social Work: Social Thought, 35*(1–2), 24–40.

Derken, D., Barker, J., McMillan, K., & Stewart, L. (2017). *Rates of current mental disorders among women offenders in CSC.* Correctional Services Canada.

Elfleet, H. (2021). Neoliberal feminised governmentality: The role and function of a post Corston Report (2007) women's centre in the north-west of England. *British Journal of Community Justice, 16*(2), 1–22.

Evans, A., & Coccoma, P. (2014). *Trauma-informed care: How neuroscience influences practice.* Routledge.

Grella, C. (1999). Women in residential drug treatment: Differences by program type and pregnancy. *Journal of Health Care for the Poor and Underserved, 10*(2), 216–229.

Fortune, C., Willis, G., & Ward, T. (2012). The rehabilitation of offenders: Reducing risk and promoting better lives. *Psychiatry, Psychology and Law, 19*(5), 646–661.

Jesso, M. (2018). *Newfoundland and Labrador correctional and community services: Deaths in custody review.* Department of Justice. Retrieved February 29, 2024, from https://www.gov.nl.ca/jps/files/publications-pdf-death-custody-review.pdf

Kilty, J. (2012). 'It's like they don't want you to get better': Psy control of women in the carceral context. *Feminism & Psychology, 22*(2), 162–182.

Maidment, M. R. (2006). *Doing time on the outside: Deconstructing the benevolent community.* University of Toronto Press.

Maruna, S. (2001). *Making good: How ex-convicts reform and rebuild their lives.* American Psychological Association.

Maruna, S., & Roy, K. (2007). Amputation or reconstruction? Notes on the concept of "knifing off" and desistance from crime. *Journal of Contemporary Criminal Justice, 23*(1), 104–124.

Matheson, F., Brazil, A., Doherty, S., & Forrester, P. (2015). A call for help: Women offenders' reflections on trauma care. *Women & Criminal Justice, 25*(4), 241–255.

O'Brien, P. (2001). *Making it in the "free world:" Women in transition from prison.* State University of New York Press.

Pearson, M., Brand, S. L., Quinn, C., Shaw, J., Maguire, M., Michie, S., Briscoe, S., Lennox, C., Stirzaker, A., Kirkpatrick, T., & Byng, R. (2015). Using realist review to inform intervention development: Methodological illustration and conceptual platform for collaborative care in offender mental health. *Implementation Science, 10*(1), 1–12.

Rutter, N., & Barr, U. (2021). Being a 'good woman': Stigma, relationships and desistance. *Probation Journal, 68*(2), 166–185.

Sieter, R. P., & Kadela, K. R. (2003). Prisoner reentry: What works, what does not, and what is promising. *Crime & Delinquency, 49*(3), 360–388.

Travis, J. (2005). *But they all come back: Facing the challenges of prisoner reentry.* The Urban Institute.

Ward, T., & Maruna, S. (2007). *Rehabilitation: Beyond the risk paradigm.* Routledge.

Ward, T. (2002). Good lives and the rehabilitation of offenders. *Aggression and Violent Behavior, 7*(5), 513–528.

World Health Organization. (2013). ROADMAP. Strengthening people-centred health systems in the WHO European Region: A framework for action towards coordinated/integrated health services delivery (CIHSD).

Zinger, I. (2014). *Reflections on conditions of confinement for federally sentenced women.* Office of Correctional Investigator.

CHAPTER 5

Continuing the Journey: Stigma and Women's Desistance

Abstract Criminalized women face multiple stigmas impacting their lives and ability to desist in profound ways. In this chapter, I explore formerly incarcerated women's experiences of intersecting stigmas and how they impact their ability to access services. Women feel discriminated against and thus have difficulties accessing essential needs such as housing and employment. Further, they feel stigma impacts when accessing health care services. Women internalize such experiences and stigma, resulting in feeling undeserving of the support and services available to them. The desistance process is relational, meaning that desisters need people in their corner to support them. Desistance, therefore, needs to be seen as a community's journey alongside the desister, providing needed support and feedback. Strategies of love, compassion, and support must replace surveillance, punishment, and prison.

Keywords Stigma · Gender · Mental health · Services · Self-worth

INTRODUCTION

The formerly incarcerated women and service providers I spoke to identified stigma as challenging for women exiting prison and beginning a path to desistance. Stigma is "an attribute that is deeply discrediting"

(Goffman, 1963, p. 30). Some individuals who experience stigma also are the target of prejudice and discrimination (Link & Phelan, 1999). For example, the stigma of a criminal record can result in difficulties finding employment due to discrimination against hiring a criminalized person. Additionally, stigma can impact reentry success in housing and community access. The result is social exclusion. Experiences of stigma, discrimination and social exclusion, an experience not uncommon to those with a criminal history, can result in an individual internalizing that stigma, causing feelings of deep shame, whereby an individual believes that there is something inherently wrong with them as a person (Gålnander, 2020; Goffman, 1963). Furthermore, the perception of stigmatization from others is a predictor of low self-esteem and dissatisfaction with life (LeBel, 2008). Thus, experiences of stigma can have a profound impact on the lives of the women interviewed.

The women I interviewed face multiple stigmatizing identities due to their criminal history, mental health, and addictions, and they have experienced discrimination due to these stigmatized identities. Moreover, stigmatizing identities among the women interact with gender and race to compound stigma.

Interviewed participants also explained how feelings of shame due to stigma caused them to feel undeserving of help, thus preventing them from seeking support in response to discrimination. Therefore, feelings of shame and the experiences of discrimination challenged their process of desistance. Desistance relies on an individual's ability to make a cognitive shift from identifying with criminal behaviour to identifying with pro-social goals and lifestyles (Giordano et al., 2002; Maruna, 2001). Formerly incarcerated women experience multiple and intersecting stigmas (LeBel, 2012) that may bar them from some forms of pro-social belonging and engagement, challenging the cognitive shift needed for desistance. Moreover, discrimination will affect former prisoners' ability to engage in practical elements of the desistance process. For example, many people with criminal histories face challenges when seeking employment (Ricciardelli & Mooney, 2018). Employment is a critical element in the desistance process (Anazodo et al., 2019) and living a pro-social life (Ricciardelli et al., 2019). However, a criminal record or history of incarceration can reduce, even limit, employment opportunities.

In the current chapter, I examine how stigma shapes the desistance process, both practically and the cognitive processes at play. First, I examine multiple stigmas (criminal record, addiction, mental health, race, and gender) and the challenges these compounding issues pose to desistance. I then explore how experiences of stigma impact women's abilities to access services that can aid in desistance. Finally, I examine women's experiences of internalized stigma and the impacts on desistance.

MULTIPLE INTERSECTING STIGMAS

During interviews with formerly imprisoned women and service providers, they identified stigma associated with criminal records, mental disorders, sex work, substance misuse, gender, and race. These multiple stigmas overlap at times, compounding the impact of other stigmas. At other times, women can engage in stigma management by revealing only partially stigmatized identities.

Gender and a Criminal Record

Both formerly incarcerated women and service providers acknowledged that gender shapes the stigma associated with a criminal record. Gender intersects with, a criminal history, to create an extra layer of stigma, resulting in criminalized women being perceived as doubly deviant, breaking the law and gender norms (Carlen, 1995; Lander, 2015). Criminalized women are seen as violating feminine norms, which dictate that women should be passive and well-behaved. Furthermore, as Rutter and Barr (2021) suggest, criminalized women often fail to live up to the notion of a "good woman," an idea imbued with white supremacist, hetero-patriarchal, and neo-liberal values. The impact of gender on a criminal record is particularly salient when women are seeking employment post-incarceration. Ana, who has been working with people with barriers to employment for 18 years, stated:

> So, I see women who have criminal histories more marginalized. And, I think, really ghettoized then into even sex work and not to say that there's anything wrong with sex work and some women want to do that. But I know some I've worked with some who get into that because it's just like, well, that's what I could get.

In Ana's experience, criminal records are barriers to employment for men. However, men are more likely to circumvent these issues by working under the table or going into traditionally male fields where a criminal record does not impact employment as much (e.g., construction, roofing, asbestos abatement). Ana also suggests that women are "ghettoized" in sex work. While she acknowledges that sex work is not inherently problematic, sex work is a problem when women feel they have no other choices. Moreover, another stigma is associated with sex work which further adds to the stigma of gender and criminality. Camilla, a service provider, asserts that sex workers, particularly street-based sex workers, face stigma through "policing approaches, through surveillance." Here, Camilla suggests that women working in the sex trade are subject to extra scrutiny from police and, thus, at risk for potential arrest.

Local communities also stigmatize sex workers, describing sex work as a safety concern for community members, but notably do not identify safety concerns for the workers. Based on alarm from citizens, Living in Community, a steering committee aimed at creating safer communities, compiled a report which included interviews with sex workers (all self-identifying as women), service providers, and community members. The report found that sex workers experienced stigma and discrimination, affecting their safety (Living in Community, 2020). For service providers Ana and Camilla, women with a criminal record engaged in sex work are battling stigmas that affect their ability to find alternate work and their safety within the available, viable work options. Sex work is quite diverse (including massage, dancing, escorting, and street-based work) and often operates on the edge of legality. While sex work is not inherently dangerous, sex work is subject to "discourses of hate," which lay the groundwork for stigma and violence against sex workers (Sanders, 2016). Thus, criminalized women are magnifying stigma due to their criminal history and engagement in sex work.

Criminalized women seeking more established employment options often struggle given that more "traditional" women's work is people-focused and in positions of trust (for example, cleaning or homecare). The existence of a criminal record stigmatizes persons as law-breakers rather than law abiders, which impedes the extension of the trust necessary to hire an individual into an employment position whether under the table or within the formal labour market. Women interviewed were acutely aware of the stigma associated with being a woman with a criminal history and how the stigma affects their access to services and finding employment. When I spoke to Jane, a formerly incarcerated woman and asked about the services she needed, she replied:

Try to help us with jobs. Being a female is harder to get a job than for a male. Being a criminal and having a criminal background, it's harder for women than for men. Because (the jobs) are more for men.

Jane recognizes the extra challenges for women with criminal records in finding employment. Previously a homecare provider, Jane felt she could not return to that kind of work with her criminal record. She believes that getting into work like construction is easier when you have a criminal record, but construction can be a challenging industry for women. Jane recognizes the importance of employment in meeting her goals for a pro-social life, consistent with researchers who find that employment positively affects desistance (Pager & Western, 2009; Roderman et al., 2016). Jane understands how stigma and discrimination will impact her ability to live a pro-social life and asks that service providers help in her goals for employment in hopes of mitigating the stigma.

Racism, Colonialism, and a Criminal Record

Like elsewhere in Canada, Indigenous people are disproportionally represented in the criminal justice system in NL. In the province, female Indigenous admissions to adult custody comprise 24% of all admissions (Malakieh, 2018) while making up 7% of the province's population (Chernikova, 2016). Marques and Monchalin (2020) assert that the mass incarceration of Indigenous women reflects patriarchal, colonial tactics of control designed to assimilate and control Indigenous women. Furthermore, they argue that because prison systems are designed for the needs of white men, current carceral systems do not address the needs of Indigenous women in prison.

I interviewed two Indigenous women. Both discussed the importance of connection to their culture and People as necessary to their healing after release from prison. However, aside from one woman stating that the language barrier was a challenge, neither specifically mentioned racism. I speculate that the two Indigenous women interviewed did not mention racism because such experiences are ingrained in their commonality that they are a way of life rather than an unusual experience for these women. Service providers, conversely, are more likely to see the systemic patterns of racism/colonialism while working with many Indigenous people. As a service provider working within the prison, many Indigenous women have told me about their experiences of racism, including name-calling, isolation, and bullying by other prisoners, but without speaking to issues of systemic racism or how such practices or experiences affect desistance. Instead, women speak about the experiences that impact their daily lives while living in prison.

One service provider interviewed identified racism as an issue for women with a criminal record when released from prison. Jackie shares:

> When we're working with people in the community and being reintegrated, I'm still hearing that they're feeling stereotyped. That they're feeling judged. That they're feeling they're experiencing racism or especially if they are visibly Indigenous, not white-passing. So yeah, I'm seeing that I'm also seeing barriers like, you know, they have a criminal record, so that impacts employment.

Jackie's words reveal the interpretation of the community members placing a "triple deviant" stigma on women identifying as Indigenous (Yeun, 2011). Criminalized Indigenous women transgress traditional notions of femininity by nature of Indigeneity and through participation in criminal activity and/or drug use (Dell & Kilty, 2013). Jackie, recognizing how stigma affects her clients, describes challenges supporting Indigenous women in obtaining employment, which she sees as a component of the process of community reentry.

Mental Health Issues and a Criminal Record

While most people living with mental health disorders do not have a criminal record, mental health disorders are prevalent among criminalized women. Incarcerated women experience high rates of mental illness, including Post-Traumatic Stress Disorder, Major Depressive Disorder, General Anxiety Disorder, substance use, Schizophrenia, and other mood and personality disorders (Brown et al., 2018; Kilty, 2012). All women interviewed self-identified with a mental health concern but not necessarily that they had been diagnosed by a mental health professional. They identified their mental health as a concern in daily living.

I found that mental illness connects and interacts with a criminal record in two ways. First, experiencing stigma and discrimination can impact mental health by exacerbating symptoms of mental disorders. Second, the ability to hide a stigmatizing identity can provide opportunities for creative stigma management.

Experiences of discrimination due to a criminal record can exacerbate psychological distress. For example, in discussing employment goals, Laura, a formerly incarcerated woman, states, "I don't know....the employment thing. It probably got a lot to do with me because I am nervous about people knowing. It's not hard to Google." Here, if uncovered, Laura worries about the stigma associated with her criminal justice involvement. Convicted of serious charges, Laura worries about potential employers searching her name on the internet, revealing news articles including pictures and details of her conviction. Laura is so anxious about employers finding out about her criminal history that she is reluctant to seek employment. Thus, the idea of disclosure amplifies the symptoms of her mental illness.

Other women shared similar experiences and described the effects of such an experience on their mental health, for instance, the stress of asking for time off to go to a probation appointment. The stress and worry about disclosing or discovering criminal history were harmful to mental health and well-being. Ricciardelli and Spencer (2014) similarly found that some sex offenders are in a constant state of apprehension and anxiety at the prospect of their crimes being revealed. While women in this study were not convicted of sex offences, their crimes carry the stigma that contributes to a precarious existence while waiting on what they see as inevitable disclosure of their crimes.

On the other hand, for some women, multiple stigmatizing identities can allow them to creatively manage disclosure, choosing to whom they can safely reveal a stigmatizing identity. For example, some women chose to hide their criminal history but presented another stigmatized identity, such as a mental disorder. At least in part, for some women, revealing they had a disorder was easier, or perhaps less stigmatizing, than revealing their criminal history. Grace provides employment support for individuals with mental health concerns. She shares a story about a client she tried to help obtain employment for over a year:

> I met with her and built that therapeutic relationship, then one day, she was like, I have to tell you something. I was like, what are you gonna tell me? She's like, I have a criminal record. I was like, oh...., now I know why you can't get a job! Why aren't you telling me this like months ago?

Grace explained that she was puzzled by her client being underemployed. Eventually, the client disclosed having a criminal record. Grace shared that her client would go for interviews and be offered the job, but she would not return once they asked for a record of conduct. Grace explains that her client was so ashamed of her criminal record that she would not disclose it to service providers whose role was to support her in her endeavours to find work. Grace's story reveals the extent of her client's shame and embarrassment tied to her criminal past, making disclosing itself a barrier to her support seeking and employment attainment. Contrastingly, she was willing to disclose her mental disorder to access employment support services. Thus, for Grace's client, the revelation of her mental disorder was less stigmatizing than her criminal record.

On the other hand, some interviewees with an incarceration history were reluctant to share their mental health histories due to poor past experiences. Erica, a formerly incarcerated woman, shares:

> My first job I went to (after leaving prison) I think that as soon as I told her (something changed). I was doing so good, but not letting her know about my personal life, about the bipolar, right? As soon as I let her know, the supervisor that I was bipolar. I was treated different. I was, you know, kind of pitied, right?

In Erica's experience, sharing about her mental disorder at her job did not go well. While her employer did not fire her, she felt that her employer treated her differently because of her mental disorder. While often, women are encouraged to disclose mental disorders as they may require accommodations, there remains the fear of discrimination. Discrimination is not always about not getting a job or losing a job but being treated differently, including being pitied. Thus, disclosing mental illness may not be an option for some women, even though they may need services or accommodations.

I observed a seeming "hierarchy of stigma" tied to the stigma's visibility. Given that some stigmatizing identities are visible, others—those that are arguably invisible—can be disclosed at the choice of the bearer or can be "outted." Both a criminal history and a mental disorder are arguably invisible. Variable among our participants was which, their criminal record or mental disorder, was more or less problematic. The ability to determine which stigmatizing identity is more impactful, combined with the choice for disclosure, is a form of stigma management. Women control the information they share, with whom they share it, and for what purposes. For instance, a criminal record is required to access some services, such as the Just Us Women's Centre or Elizabeth Fry societies. For other services, such as some employment support programmes, a mental health disorder is a prerequisite. Thus, some women have a choice about which stigmatizing identity to disclose.

STIGMA IMPACTING ACCESS TO SERVICES

Basic Needs

Stigma and resulting discrimination associated with a criminal record are widely recognized to have impacts on basic needs such as housing, employment, and relationships. Most women felt that stigma was inescapable as their criminal history was easily known. Women have stated that discrimination and stigma are a reality in living in a small town—Lilian shares, "It's nothing but trouble out in (town redacted). Everybody knows your business, and what they don't know, they make up. I'll visit, but I won't live there again." For Lilian, the idea that everyone talks about her in a stigmatizing manner means that she cannot live in her hometown again. The inability to live in her hometown limited her social network and meant that she lost her housing.

However, living in the city does not necessarily mean anonymity. Robyn states, "Sometimes I just find the stigma of being on probation [is daunting]. Having to go to an appointment and having to get time off work for that." Robyn has always been able to find work as she works in an industry receptive to hiring people with criminal records. However, she still experiences stigma when needing to go to mandatory probation appointments because of the time off work required. These experiences of stigma impact women's motivation to seek housing and employment for fear of facing more discrimination.

When women do seek housing, they are likely to face discrimination. When asked about the challenges of being released from prison, Judy stated, "I guess landlords don't want to rent to people like us." Jackie, a service provider, shared difficulties for women she has worked with:

> Even getting references for housing? Well, who's your last landlord? My last landlord was two years ago. Yeah, but I want your most recent one.

> Where were you living? I was actually incarcerated, and so right away, right away, you just lost your housing.

Housing is challenging to obtain while in prison in preparation for release. When released, women face barriers in meeting their most basic housing needs due, at least in part, to the stigma associated with a criminal record and incarceration.

In addition to housing, another basic need is relationships with family, friends, and the community in which one lives. Relationships provide emotional support and a sense of belonging. A feeling of isolation post-prison is common for many formerly incarcerated individuals (Nugent & Schinkel, 2016). Women reported having difficulties connecting with the community due to their criminal past. Sarah states:

> Yeah, and I find no matter you could do a thousand good things, but they always remember you for the bad. And say another thing too, if I wanted to do volunteer work. I can't even do that because I got to have a criminal check.

Sarah here is aware that people in her life and community stigmatize her due to her criminal record. She finds stigma challenging because she wants to be involved in the community through volunteer work but feels that a criminal record will prevent her. The desire to give back to the community was common for the women interviewed. Most stated that they would like to do something that meaningfully contributes to their community as they know they have "taken" something from the community due to criminal activity. However, all women recognized that the stigma associated with a criminal record might challenge their efforts to give back. Women did not even try to volunteer as they believed a criminal record would prohibit any volunteer activities. Feeling stigmatized becomes paralysing, meaning that women will not engage in any activities, such as searching for employment or volunteer work, for fear of stigmatization.

The need to give back suggests that the process of desistance involves repairing harm done. Maruna (2001) found that desisters were focused on giving back to others and wanted to accomplish or have "something to show" for their lives. As Sarah's example shows, McNeil and Maruna (2007) suggest that the current manifestation of the criminal justice system impedes the ability to give back. The stigma associated with a criminal record impedes her ability to participate fully in the desistance process, which requires meaningful participation in her community.

Women also face less formal discrimination and stigmatization from community members, friends, and family. My conversation with Lilian explored informal stigmatization.

Amy: You feel like people are talking about you?
Lilian: Yeah, like Lilian done this and she done that and what is she doing in this area? Yeah. No, I just did not feel comfortable there, you know.

Lilian feels excluded from her home community, which is small. Although she believes that people are talking about her and the crime she committed—her crime was high profile in the local media- Lilian has few meaningful relationships with people in her life where she feels non-judgemental support. She goes on to say:

Yeah, supports are the big thing. I think...You know, I know personally for me. (Supports) would be somebody like I could just go to and sit down and they understand like, you know. They're not judging me for what I've been through, what I'm going through. And there is a lot more people like me. They really do need support to help get through daily life.

Lilian's words highlight the challenges in developing relationships and supports. Lilian wants someone to be able to confide in, who will understand and accept her without judgement. Unfortunately, she does not have supportive relationships outside of professional supports as she feels that professionals do not judge her. Judy, too, felt that professionals provided non-judgemental support to women in prison. In talking to Judy about what supports helped when incarcerated, she states:

They didn't have any self-worth. And you guys (Stella's Circle staff) gave them that. And that it's worth something. No matter what you've done, no matter what your background you're a human being, you're loved. Because there's nothing worse. I can't think of any other feeling that's harder than feeling unloved.

Judy states that being treated like a human being and being loved is essential in moving towards a pro-social life. However, without professionals visiting the prison, women often do not experience these feelings of acceptance.

Nevertheless, women need relationships beyond those provided by professionals. They need to be able to connect with family and friends. The ability to connect can be challenging for some women due to conditions placed on them by the criminal justice system. For example, women's parole conditions often prohibit associating with others involved in the criminal justice system (Turnbull & Hannah-Moffat, 2009). While parole officers will usually approve contact with other criminalized individuals while receiving services in professional settings, some women may still worry about how it looks to their parole officer. Service provider Ellen suggests that some women may not use her services because they fear what is reported to parole, including associating with other women accessing services. She states that some women fear that service-providing agencies are seen as "A good place to get your drugs. It's a good place to get back into the scene. [Service providers] know you a lot, and they can report different things." Prohibiting association with other criminalized women means that the connections made at service agencies (or in prison) cannot continue in the community, limiting social connections and furthering isolation. Insisting that women only form relationships with pro-social individuals ignores the stigma associated with a criminal record impeding developing relationships.

Most women I interviewed did not identify a robust social support network outside of professionals and agencies. However, many women were motivated to access services such as the Just Us Women's Centre due to the availability of social activities. Women accessing social events at the Just Us Women's Centre know that the events will be safe and sober, enabling them to meet others with similar desistance goals. Lillian shares, "It's nice to get out and come and visit on Monday's social group. You come here, and there's nobody looking down on you, hmm you're not... I'm not singled out as a person." Lillian feels that the social group is a safe place because she is not stigmatized or "looked down on." She sees the value of social connections.

Katie emphasized the importance of engaging socially. She states, "There is just so much out in the world. And I was in a basement for so many years." She credited having a group of friends to engage in activities such as hikes, a fire on the beach, or going to a movie as a means to abstain from drug use and move forward in her life.

If women cannot or are reluctant to access basic needs such as housing, employment, or relationships due to stigma, desistance is increasingly difficult. Participants are very aware of the stigma associated with a criminal record, substance use, mental disorders, and gender. They had many experiences whereby stigma impacted their attempts to engage in community, work, or obtain housing. Interviewees maintained they were committed to a crime-free life and not returning to prison. However, without adequate housing, opportunities for employment, and supportive relationships, the desistance journey is fraught with difficulties and, for some, may seem impossible.

Specific Agencies

Stigma can also be associated with agencies that provide services to particular populations, such as those with criminal records or substance use. Ricciardelli and Moir (2013) found that stigma was attached to a particular unit in prison that protected sex offenders. However, while non-sex offenders may be on the same unit, the stigma attached to the unit extends to any prisoner on the unit. Structural stigma[1] is connected to an institutional structure that reinforces the stigma of anyone associated with that particular stigmatized unit. Ricciardelli and Moir (2013) found that stigma attached to the institutional structure reinforced and intensified stigma. I found a similar structural stigma associated with institutions and services that work with addicted or criminalized populations. For example, some women are reluctant to access services from some agencies to avoid interacting with other people accessing services at the agency. For example, when asked why some women may not access services. Gloria stated:

---

[1] I am using the term structural stigma here as used by Ricciardelli and Moir (2013), who identify specific stigma attached to particular structures, such as a prison unit. I recognize that structural stigma has also been defined by Hannem and Bruckert (2012) as "the result of a carefully calculated decision at an institutional or bureaucratic level to manage a particular population..." (p. 24).

Yeah. Yeah, and with you guys (a women serving agency), you know, some women might not want to come because they're intimidated by other women. For years, I didn't like women at all. Like, well, (I felt) you're all fucking vindictive. You're all like, stab you in the back. Yeah, two-faced.

Gloria takes a specific attitude towards women whom she sees as untrustworthy. Her attitude towards women may be an example of internalized sexism that forms hostility towards other women (Bearman et al., 2009). Given that women are subject to stigmatization, some women turn to blame other women for their own marginalization, suggesting, as Gloria does, that women are "two-faced" and "back-stabbers." Blaming other women allows one to view themselves as not a part of that marginalized group and thus feel that one is not subject to the same stigma and discrimination (Cowan, 2000). Thus, Gloria sees other women as the back-stabbers and does not count herself among them. She is worthy of trust because she situates herself outside of the stigmatized group. Therefore, given that she views other women negatively, Gloria does not want to participate in a service where she will have to engage with other women.

Additionally, while she does not explicitly state that she does not trust *criminalized* women, Gloria references women who attend a programme designed for criminalized women of which Gloria is a part. Thus, part of the reluctance to trust women may be the internalization of stigma about criminalized people prevalent in general society. Furthermore, researchers have found that incarcerated women report that their relationships in prison are fraught with betrayal, rumours, and conflict (Greer, 2000; Trammell, 2009). Thus, Gloria's assertion that women are "back-stabbers" may be based on a history of relationships with other criminalized women, creating problems when trying to access support in the future.

Accessing services for criminalized women might be a barrier for some trying to distance themselves from other criminalized women. Some service providers echoed the sentiment, stating that they were reluctant to refer women to an agency for criminalized women. Faye, a service provider, explains:

So one of the things is that Stella's Circle is one of the main referral sources, but for some of the women, they don't want to come here because they don't want to see certain people that they have been inside with. They don't want to be faced with the temptation, so it might do a referral that's an Eastern Health referral that, from my own experience, I would know that there is not a high criminal element in that group. Yeah, so it doesn't sound very nice, but just remove them from the (criminalized) people.

Faye's statement echoes others' words about internalized stigma. In her experience, clients want to distance themselves from stigmatized groups to disassociate themselves from a marginalized population—a movement that resonates with desistance theory and processes. Maruna and Roy (2007) suggest that "knifing off" the past may be a part of early desistance when it is essential to distance from people who may influence a return to old behaviours.

Likewise some women indicated that they did not want to be associated with people living a particular lifestyle, such as those involved with drugs/alcohol or crime. For instance, Maggie, a formerly incarcerated woman, does not "want to be involved with people who are trouble. I stopped drinking and smoking." Maggie associates drinking and smoking with "people who are trouble," utilizing stereotypes surrounding substance abuse. Although Maggie has a history of substance use, she separates herself from the stereotypes of substance users. The separation may prohibit her access to services for her history of substance misuse as she does not want to be associated with other substance users. Maggie is engaged in desistance processes whereby she separates herself from her old life, her old self. However, limiting her access to services to avoid "those people" also limits her ability to get support in envisioning a replacement self and meeting future goals. Maggie identified that isolation and loneliness were problems for her; thus, limiting her social networks can exacerbate isolation.

In addition to identifying stigma due to who else may access particular services, many women identified feeling stigmatized and discriminated against when using formal, government-based services. Most women interviewed did not access services at institution-based mental health and addiction services. Most women stated that institution-based services "weren't for them." Service providers stated that many women shared with them that they had experienced prejudice and discrimination from mental health professionals working within the formalized health care system. Vivian, a service provider, explained that many women she works with are reluctant to share their circumstances, such as being involved in sex work or crime, due to a fear of judgement. She shares that she has seen clients "dismissed for certain things, or labelled as drug-seeking or as resistant to treatment."

Likewise, Ellen, a service provider, noted that criminalized women are treated differently in her experience because they are perceived as "against the stereotype of what a female should be." When I asked Ellen about barriers that prevent criminalized women from accessing services, she stated:

> I do think probably the number one barrier is that generally, women in prison are just not cute, and society doesn't like them. They are not endearing. They're not the stereotypical feminine little girl that fits the mould. They are generally rough and ready. They use harsh language. They've done things people don't like. They have tried to be a survivor and are generally unlikeable in lots of ways. And then we know that if you have people like that, often, it's hard to go above and beyond. They can be quite mean at times as a means of survival, and I think that that is often what prevents them from getting help.

Ellen states here many criminalized women are survivors, which affects how they interact with others (e.g., they may not be polite or "likable"). She posits that such interactions can alienate some service providers in more formal settings. Ellen suggests that service providers need to go "above and beyond" with their efforts to provide needed help for criminalized women. However, given the stigma associated with criminalized women and behaviour that may validate the stigma, Ellen implies that service providers are unwilling to put in the extra effort. For example, the lack of effort can look like strictly adhering to policies that discharge clients after missed appointments when there may be room for flexibility.

In addition to stigma and discrimination experienced by criminalized women in formal settings, Gloria, a formerly incarcerated woman, identified problems with NL Health Service's documentation policies; "There's a lot of paperwork. They keep records of everything they do, right." As a woman who has been involved in the criminal justice system for a long time, Gloria is aware that notes from her involvement with mental health professionals can be subpoenaed to court. Moreover, documentation from mental health professionals often contributes to labelling individuals with mental disorders, strengthening attached stereotypes and associated stigma. These policies of documentation and labelling can challenge the desistance process. Envisioning a replacement self is difficult when interactions with professionals imply your history of criminal activity, which may be related to mental health and addiction, will be attached to your name and accessed by other treatment providers within NL Health Services. Grace, a service provider, provided an example of a client trying to access psychiatric services but was termed "pill seeking" because of a criminal past and was denied treatment.

These examples demonstrate how some service providers judge a criminal past. It seems that some service providers struggle to see that some criminalized individuals are on a desistance journey, trying to distance themselves from their criminal history and envision a future self. Some service providers stated that people with criminal histories refuse to "take responsibility" for their actions because they speak about their criminal history as "not really them." Some service providers see that "knifing off" the past is a means for criminalized women to refuse responsibility for their past actions. For a woman trying to desist by separating herself from her past, it seems she cannot escape her documented history. Desistance is relational; a part of the process requires others to see the new replacement self (Nugent & Schinkel, 2016). Given these experiences with some institutions, the desistance process (i.e., the new placement self) is not seen.

INTERNALIZING STIGMA: FEELING NOT DESERVING

After experiencing stigma and discrimination from communities, professionals, potential landlords, employers, and family, individuals often turn stigma inward and start to believe that they deserve poor treatment from others (Moore et al., 2016). When asked why some women do not reach out for help, Joy and I had this conversation:

Joy: because they don't want to be downgraded? You don't want to make people feel like that. (Like) you're stupid, and that you don't deserve the help. That was me years ago. Okay, I'd say, oh, I don't deserve that.

Amy: Oh, okay. You felt like you didn't deserve help?

Joy: Even now, at times, like I literally has to tell myself. Yeah, you deserve what you got. So I dearly love having my own apartment.

Here, Joy explains that criminalized women feel "downgraded" through interactions with others, particularly professionals who are supposed to provide help. The degrading interaction with others is the process of disintegrative shaming, as proposed by Braithwaite (1989). Criminalized women are treated as if they are bad people rather than good people who have done a bad deed. Disintegrative shaming treats criminalized people as inherently bad and does not promote rehabilitation of the bad behaviour but instead contributes to the cycle of criminal acts.

Feedback from others fuels the internalized stigma and shame. Most women expressed that their families or other people in their lives do not let them forget their criminal past or other stigmatizing factors (such as addiction or engaging in sex work). Judy shares, "My family still to this day, and I'm going to be (age redacted) in a few months, and they're still doing it. Yeah, still going back to 'you were an exotic dancer. You were an alcoholic'." Likewise, Joy relayed:

Joy: It's scary. I'll tell you about this morning. I was after getting out of the shower. So, of course, I'm wrapped up in towels, and there's a knock on the front door. And I said who is it? And he said sheriff's officer. And I said, well, you better hang on now. I got to go put on something. Yeah, and it wasn't for me at all. They were looking for the woman in the front part of my building.

Amy: That was scary for you to have them come to your door? It brings stuff back?

Joy: Oh, my sister was out on the front doorstep behind (the sheriff's officer), and she said, 'what did she do now?'

Amy: It sounds like that's a big part of it for you is that people kind of keep bringing it up to you a little bit.

Joy: Yeah. If I do anything wrong sometimes with my sisters. Yeah. Yeah. They bring it up, bring it up, bring it up, bring it up and rehash it.

Judy and Joy's stories reveal how family members continually bring up past criminal events, making it challenging to move past the stigma of their past actions. The reminders contribute to internalized stigma and feelings of shame. Joy states that they "bring it up, bring it up," continually reminding women of their wrongdoing. What is more, the families of these women do not engage women in discussing what they are doing well or how they have changed. Consequently, women have trouble moving on to a replacement self and suffer the shame of reminders of the past. The desistance process involves envisioning a replacement self, a self engaging in pro-social activities. The process of envisioning the replacement self will undoubtedly be challenged if the family continually reminds the individual of their old self in a stigmatizing fashion, such as the examples provided by Joy and Judy. An alternative would be families and others reminding desisters of their past in a positive manner (e.g., "Look how far you have come").

Desisters could feel supported and see that others believe in them. I asked Laura what she needed to make the changes she did in her life. She needed support, "someone to say, yes, you can do that. It's nice to have people who give you that confidence that you don't really have in yourself all the time." As Laura states, she does not always have the confidence to continue to make positive changes in her life. She relies on others for support and to remind her of how far she has come. Using a positive support model to help desisters see how far they have come means that reminders of the past can help cement that the old way of life is no longer desirable. Supportive people can help desisters reflect on their criminal past to promote desistance, suggesting to the desister that you are not that past person anymore.

The process of desistance is relational; it involves the acceptance and recognition of desistance by other people (Nugent & Schinkel, 2016). Rutter and Barr (2021) suggest that positive relationships which help women to challenge their feelings of shame are essential to women's desistance processes. Unfortunately, for many women interviewed, people in their lives do not recognize changes made or assume that the changes are a momentary blip and the person will return to their old, deviant self.

On the other hand, do shame and reminders of a troubled past prompt people not to commit the same mistakes/acts? As Katie shares here: "Shame's a big part of it. You don't want to face the reality of it. Yeah, or re-live it, but you got to re-live it and get through in order to get past it." Katie believes that the process of desistance, referred to as getting "past it," involves living with and dealing with the shame that comes with criminal acts. Braithwaite (1989) suggests two types of shaming: reintegrative and stigmatizing. In reintegrative shaming, a person is shamed for the acts committed and maintains a sense of worth. In stigmatizing shaming, both the person and the act are deemed shameful. Reintegrative shaming is more helpful than stigmatizing shaming in the desistance process. Katie and other women in the current study are subject to stigmatizing shaming from family, friends, and the community at large. However, amid stigmatizing shaming, there are some messages of reintegrative shaming. These reintegrative messages are from professionals who suggest that Katie needs to deal with her past to move on with her life.

Katie's quote suggests that she believes a part of her is worthy of moving on from her past. In other words, Katie does not wholly tie her identity to her past actions. Instead, she strives to become a new person once she can "get past it." Katie's desire to confront her past exemplifies what Maruna (2001) terms tragic optimism, the idea that something good, a new life, can come from a troubled past. Moreover, Katie can see that she has control over her destiny, a component of desistance (Maruna, 2001). Katie actively engaged in therapy as a part of her mission to work through her history and "get past it." She was also actively engaged in social activities with supportive friends who knew about her past and supported her by engaging in pro-social activities. Katie was making plans to return to school and find employment. In addition to adding these new things to her life, Katie had a positive attitude and said she was happy. She reflected on her past and gained strengths, such as resiliency, that would support her in her new life. Engaged in the process of creating a new life, Katie was aware that stigma could impact opportunities. However, she displayed optimism that through her own hard work, the support of professionals and her positive friend network, she would move past her criminal history towards a pro-social life.

Conclusion

Multiple stigmas affect an individual's ability to desist. Practical elements of desisting, such as obtaining safe housing, meaningful employment, and supportive relationships, are impacted by stigma. Criminal records impede finding housing or employment because landlords or employers discriminate. In addition to the stigma associated with a criminal record, women have experienced stigma due to mental health disorders, drug use, race, and gender. Again, these experiences impact their ability to desist from criminal behaviour. For example, participants said they stopped looking for employment because they knew the potential for discrimination. Many women stated that the potential for discrimination and stigmatization kept them from asking for help from service providers because they felt undeserving. Others did not want to engage with particular agencies due to the stigma associated with the population served by that agency.

Therefore, women stated that the experiences of discrimination prevented them from utilizing professional services, such as therapy and employment counselling, that may enable the desistance process. Women needed help to make changes in their lives, but that stigma and shame made reaching out for help challenging. Service providers can help with desistance. The desistance process relies on an identity shift from a criminal identity towards a pro-social identity. Service providers can aid clients in making the shift. However, feeling undeserving means that women did not always acquire or seek the needed help. Furthermore, women's experiences of stigma and discrimination result in isolation, impeding relational elements of desistance, such as finding new social groups. As a result, women find themselves in liminal spaces between distancing themselves from their old lifestyle, including friends, and unable to create a new lifestyle, including new friendships.

A crucial part of the desistance process is for others to see the change to self. Discrimination that formerly incarcerated women experience invalidates the changes made because they know that they are stigmatized as that old, criminal version of themselves. Maruna (2001) emphasizes the importance of having "someone (who) believes in you and makes you realize your value" (p. 96). Many women have someone who believes in them: service providers, counsellors, and prison staff. However, others in their lives, such as family, counteract these messages. Family and friends may be wary of changes and wait for the old behaviour to return. The challenge is helping people, both those directly engaged in the process and their family and friends, understand that the desistance process is not linear. Frequently, people will re-offend or return to old behaviours before fully making the identity shift to a pro-social lifestyle. The cyclical desistance/persistence process may be exacerbated if the individual feels no one supports the changes. Thus, it becomes essential to help family, friends, and the public understand how they can support desistence by supporting change.

On the other hand, in her study of desisting women, Gålnander (2020) found that when others relayed positive messages to women about their pasts, some women perceived these comments as insults or backhanded compliments. She found that when others recognized women in her study as improving their lives, they continued to feel like "deviant outsiders" as if their past would tarnish them forever (Gålnander, 2020, p. 1316). She stated that being recognized as having made changes for women in her study, being "better than before," confirmed that actions in their past were wrong or bad. I did not find similar experiences for women in my study. They stated they needed validation from others to acknowledge growth, change, and support to keep going. Women in my study recognized the possibility of sliding back into old behaviours and felt that positive encouragement, including recognition that they are better than they were before, would aid in the desistance process and lessen the impacts of stigma from others who do not see the changes. The contrast between the current study and Gålnander's (2020) study may be due to where women are in the desistance process. Hearing positive reinforcement regarding changes can be validating for women at the beginning stages of desistance. However, for women who have desisted for years, rehashing the past, even intended as positive, might be an unpleasant reminder of their old self. That being said, women in my study were at varying stages of desistance, with one woman having desisted successfully for over 15 years.

Braithwaite (2000) suggests that shame can be helpful in desistance. He proposes that reintegrative shaming is a tool that can be used to promote rehabilitation and desistance. Reintegrative shaming is respectful communication that tells wrongdoers that they have done an immoral act but remain a good person. However, women in the current study suggested that shame is a barrier to asking for help as they felt undeserving. Furthermore, their treatment by some was dehumanizing. They have experienced some service providers (including prison staff) who treated them with dignity and "like a human." However, that women feel it is noteworthy that people treat them with dignity is sad and disturbing. The noteworthiness is indicative that women in the current study usually do not expect to be treated humanely. Thus, most women have experienced shaming as a tool that continues to punish them long after they complete their formal sentence.

Walking the path to desistance is a tightrope, trying to distance oneself from the past while accepting responsibility for the past actions and knowing that others do not understand the journey. There is a threat of stigmatization in accessing some supports. There is a dilemma in knowing that some support networks may not help because of encountering others who may be triggers to revert to the old behaviour. Women need peers but are also likely to discriminate against others who are on the same journey towards desistance. Desistance is complicated, contradictory, and confusing.

Formerly incarcerated women's experiences of stigma and discrimination can make the process of desistance seem futile. The desistance process requires a cognitive shift, thinking about criminal activity in a way that no longer feels useful, viable, or a part of one's life. Furthermore, desistance requires thinking about a new life, not only a move away from a criminal lifestyle but a move towards a better, pro-social life. Like other formerly incarcerated individuals (Sheppard & Ricciardelli, 2016), women in the current study have modest goals for living a "good life." Women want to engage with their families, including children. They want to have friends and be active in their communities. Many women would like to work or further their education. Women want to live in safe, affordable housing that they can call home. These are achievable goals that anyone would share. However, many women in the current study feel that these goals are impeded due to stigma and discrimination. Women feel "marked" by stigma, and therefore, some feel undeserving of the simple goals identified. Others feel that the mark is so visible that others will always judge them, making employment and other community engagement impossible.

Desistance is an individual's journey through a cognitive process requiring meaningful self-reflection. The desistance journey does not occur in isolation but rather in a context whereby judgement, stigma, and discrimination impact self-perception. Desistance, therefore, needs to be seen as a community's journey alongside the desister, providing needed support and feedback. I echo the call from Hart (2017) and Rutter and Barr (2021), who suggest that love, compassion, and support must be central to supporting women's desistance. Strategies of love, compassion, and support must replace surveillance, punishment, and prison.

REFERENCES

Anazodo, K. S., Ricciardelli, R., & Chan, C. (2019). Employment after incarceration: Managing a socially stigmatized identity. *Equality, Diversity and Inclusion: An International Journal, 38*(5), 564–582.

Bearman, S., Korobov, N., & Thorne, A. (2009). The fabric of internalized sexism. *Journal of Integrated Social Sciences, 1*(1), 10–47.

Braithwaite, J. (1989). *Crime, shame and reintegration.* Cambridge University Press.

Braithwaite, J. (2000). Shame and criminal justice. *Canadian Journal of Criminology, 42*(3), 281–298.

Brown, G. P., Barker, J., McMillan, K., Norman, R., Derkzen, D., Stewart, L. A., & Wardrop, K. (2018). *Prevalence of mental disorder among federally sentenced women offenders: In-custody and intake samples.* Correctional Services Canada. Retrieved December 4, 2021, from https://www.csc-scc.gc.ca/research/r-420-en.shtml

Carlen, P. (1995). 'Virginia, criminology and the anti-social control of women' In T. Blumberg & S. Cohen (Eds.), *Punishment and social control* (pp. 117–132). Aldine de Gruyter.

Chernikova, E. (2016). *Aboriginal peoples: Fact sheet for Newfoundland and Labrador.* Social and Aboriginal Status Statistics Division, Statistics Canada. Retrieved May 14, 2021, from https://www150.statcan.gc.ca/n1/en/pub/89-656-x/89-656-x2016002-eng.pdf?st=gYI-cYGU

Cowan, G. (2000). Women's hostility toward women and rape and sexual harassment myths. *Violence against Women, 6*(3), 238–246.

Dell, C. A., & Kilty, J. M. (2013). The creation of the expected aboriginal woman drug offender in Canada: Exploring relations between victimization, punishment, and cultural identity. *International Review of Victimology, 19*(1), 51–68.

Gålnander, R. (2020). 'Shark in the fish tank': Secrets and stigma in relational desistance from crime. *The British Journal of Criminology, 60*(5), 1302–1319.

Giordano, P., Cernkovich, S. A., & Rudolph, J. L. (2002). Gender, crime, and desistance: Toward a theory of cognitive transformation. *American Journal of Sociology, 107*(4), 990–1064.

Goffman, E. (1963). *Stigma: Notes on the management of spoiled identity.* Simon and Schuster.

Greer, K. R. (2000). The changing nature of interpersonal relationships in a women's prison. *The Prison Journal, 80*(4), 442–468.

Hannem, S., & Bruckert, C. (2012). *Stigma revisited: Implications of the mark.* University of Ottawa Press.

Hart, E. L. (2017). Prisoners post release: The need for a 'critical desistance. In E. L. Hart & van Ginneken (Eds.), *New perspectives on desistance: Theoretical and empirical developments* (pp. 267–288). Palgrave MacMillan.

Kilty, J. (2012). 'It's like they don't want you to get better': Psy control of women in the carceral context. *Feminism & Psychology, 22*(2), 162–182.

Lander, I. (2015). Gender, ageing and drug use: A post-structural approach to the life course. *British Journal of Criminology, 55*(2), 270–285.

LeBel, T. P. (2008). Perceptions of and responses to stigma. *Sociology Compass, 2*(2), 409–432.

LeBel, T. P. (2012). If one doesn't get you, another one will: Formerly incarcerated persons' perceptions of discrimination. *The Prison Journal, 92*(1), 63–87.

Link, B. G., & Phelan, J. C. (1999). The labeling theory of mental disorder (II): The consequences of labeling. In A. V. Horwitz & T. L. Scheid (Eds.), *A handbook for the study of mental health: Social contexts, theories, and systems* (pp. 361–376). Cambridge University Press.

Living in Community. (2020). *Community dialogues report*. Retrieved March 2, 2024, from https://happycity.ca/2021/01/04/living-in-community-st-johns-releases-new-report/

Malakieh, J. (2018). *Adult and youth correctional statistics in Canada, 2016/2017*. Canadian Centre for Justice Statistics.

Marques, O., & Monchalin, L. (2020). The mass incarceration of indigenous women in Canada: A colonial tactic of control and assimilation. In L. George, A. Norris, A. Deckert, & J. Tauri (Eds.), *Neo-colonial injustice and the mass imprisonment of Indigenous women* (pp. 79–102). Palgrave Macmillan.

Maruna, S. (2001). *Making good: How ex-convicts reform and rebuild their lives*. American Psychological Association.

Maruna, S., & Roy, K. (2007). Amputation or reconstruction? Notes on the concept of "knifing off" and desistance from crime. *Journal of Contemporary Criminal Justice, 23*(1), 104–124.

McNeill, F., & Maruna, S. (2007). Giving up and giving back: Desistance, generativity and social work with offenders. In G. McIvor & P. Raynor (Eds.), *Developments in social work with offenders* (pp. 224–339). Jessica Kingsley Publishers.

Moore, K. E., Tangney, J. P., & Stuewig, J. B. (2016). The self-stigma process in criminal offenders. *Stigma and Health, 1*(3), 206–224.

Nugent, B., & Schinkel, M. (2016). The pains of desistance. *Criminology and Criminal Justice, 16*(5), 568–584.

Pager, D., & Western, B. (2009). *Investigating prisoner reentry: The impact of conviction status on the employment prospects of young men*. National Institute of Justice.

Ricciardelli, R., & Mooney, T. (2018). The decision to disclose: Employment after prison. *Journal of Offender Rehabilitation, 57*(6), 343–366.

Ricciardelli, R., & Moir, M. (2013). Stigmatized among the stigmatized: Sex offenders in Canadian penitentiaries. *Canadian Journal of Criminology and Criminal Justice, 55*(3), 353–386.

Ricciardelli, R., Sheppard, A., & Mooney, T. (2019). Employment reentry: Unpacking the experiences and recommendations of former federal Canadian prisoners. *Advancing Corrections: Journal of the International Corrections and Prisons Association, 7*, 97–112.

Ricciardelli, R., & Spencer, D. (2014). Exposing sex offenders: Precarity, abjection and violence in the Canadian federal prison system. *British Journal of Criminology, 54*(3), 428–448.

Rodermond, E., Kruttschnitt, C., Slotboom, A.-M., & Bijleveld, C. C. (2016). Female desistance: A review of the literature. *European Journal of Criminology, 13*(1), 3–28.

Rutter, N., & Barr, U. (2021). Being a 'good woman': Stigma, relationships and desistance. *Probation Journal, 68*(2), 166–185.

Sanders, T. (2016). Inevitably violent? Dynamics of space, governance, and stigma in understanding violence against sex workers. In *Special issue: Problematizing prostitution—Critical research and scholarship.* Emerald Group Publishing Limited.

Sheppard, A., & Ricciardelli, R. (2016). Let's dance: Exploring dance programs in prisons in the context of reentry. *Journal of Community Corrections, 25*(4), 9–15.

Trammell, R. (2009). Relational violence in women's prison: How women describe interpersonal violence and gender. *Women & Criminal Justice, 19*(4), 267–285.

Turnbull, S., & Hannah-Moffat, K. (2009). Under these conditions: Gender, parole and the governance of reintegration. *The British Journal of Criminology, 49*(4), 532–551.

Yuen, F. (2011). "I've never been so free in all my life:" Healing through aboriginal ceremonies in prison. *Leisure/loisir, 35*(2), 97–113.

CHAPTER 6

Supporting Women's Ways Forward

Abstract In this chapter, based on interviews with formerly incarcerated women and service providers, I explore potential policy, service, and practice changes to bolster desistence journeys. Recommendations include a hybrid halfway house model, re-framing harm reduction, ensuring criminalized women have services tailored to their unique needs and means to address stigma within existing services.

Keywords Housing · Harm reduction · Stigma · Services · Service providers

INTRODUCTION

After examining what formerly incarcerated women and services providers say about the desistance process, what can be done to support women along their desistance journey? A key piece is listening to what women say about their lives, experiences of prison, and desistance. During interviews with service providers who work with criminalized women, I discovered they knew little about what goes on in prison. Given that most service providers I interviewed do not provide direct service delivery within the prison, my finding should be unsurprising. Foucault (1995) observed that punishment has become hidden; what was once a public spectacle is now locked behind bars and secretive. Moreover, researchers seeking access to prisons face multiple barriers to accessing closed institutions (Reiter, 2014). Lack of access to prisons means challenges in understanding what happens in prisons for those who have never been imprisoned or worked within the system. However, information about what happens in prison trickles out from those who have been to prison. They are the experts regarding prison life. Here, I have shared that formerly incarcerated women share their experiences of prison. Given that prison can be a mystery to those outside supporting women coming out of prison, it is crucial to hear women's voices so that service providers can advocate and provide the services needed.

Both women who have experienced prison and the service providers who support them shared how women leaving prison can be better supported in achieving their goals of desistance. In the current chapter, I examine how former prisoners' ideas and suggestions can influence policy and practice. First, I examine policy implications for housing, including halfway houses for women. I then examine harm-reduction practices and how these practices help and hinder women's desistance processes. I follow this by discussing specialized services aimed at criminalized women before addressing the stigma associated with criminalized women. I conclude the chapter by reflecting on my social work practice.

HOUSING

The lack of safe, affordable housing was brought forth as an issue that impacts women leaving prison. Several research participants suggested the need for a dedicated halfway house for women in NL. There is a dearth of literature that examines halfway houses' effectiveness generally and even less that examines how halfway houses impact women. However, there is an assumption that halfway houses are helpful. Given that women need a place to live after being released from prison, it may seem that the development of a halfway house for women in NL is logical. However, a halfway house is not necessarily the answer, as there are problematic aspects of halfway houses as an extension of the prison system.

A challenge in providing housing for women post-prison is the tension between supporting women in their needs and staff's accountability to prison structures if women are on parole or a temporary absence. Maier (2020a) suggests that halfway houses have become integral to the Canadian state-wide punishment system. She argues that the halfway house's enmeshment in state punishment has led to a widening nature of workers' supervision responsibilities. Halfway house staff enforce rules, report resident infractions, and progress to parole officers and prison officials (Maier, 2020b). Halfway house staff can then contribute somewhat to difficulties for released prisoners.

Conceptualized as the "pains of release," there are many, often invisible, challenges and punishments accompanying release from prison (Travis, 2002). These challenges after release from prison include scrutiny from the staff at halfway houses, which some women report as adding stress on release due to the high level of monitoring from staff (McKendy & Ricciardelli, 2020). Monitoring from halfway house staff prioritizes requirements from parole officers and prison staff, which some releasees feel is detrimental to their own goals, such as mothering or employment (Opsal, 2012). Halfway houses are extensions of the carceral system where risk management is the priority.

Another challenge for women in halfway houses is acquiring needed support for drug and alcohol addictions. Recovery from drug and alcohol use is often cyclical, meaning that people in recovery return to misusing substances while also exploring how recovery can work for them. Slips and relapses back into drug/alcohol use are an expected part of recovery. However, the use of alcohol and drugs may violate parole conditions, which put halfway house staff in the position to report what they see. Given that staff are required to report drug and alcohol use, women may be reluctant to disclose use, impeding their recovery. They may not seek support for fear of being reported as a parole violation. A critical tenet of the harm-reduction approach to substance use is that services must be user-friendly and relevant to the service user (MacMaster, 2004). For criminalized women, services must be flexible in treating substance use, recognizing that a slip back into drug use is a part of recovery. This philosophy may conflict with the duties required by halfway house employees.

Given that halfway house staff are responsible for reporting to parole officers and prison officials, Maier (2020a) suggests that researchers and practitioners consider halfway houses "open prisons," allowing us to critique halfway houses as part of the penal system. Thus, the suggestion to think about halfway houses as an "open prison" problematizes suggestions for women's housing when released from prison. We must consider the implications for released women; halfway houses are not merely a housing option. Instead, they are an extension of prison whereby women are still under carceral control. On the other hand, the province of NL lacks a halfway house for women only, and many women I interviewed stated that they need a women-only halfway house. Furthermore, as discussed in Chapter 2, many women shared that prison helped manage their addiction. Can the penal nature of a halfway house be helpful as women transition to the community?

The current reality is that CSC and NLCCW often require women who wish to be released on parole or temporary absence to live in a staffed facility. Without a halfway house, women's options are limited, and thus, some women stay in prison longer than necessary. Therefore, although halfway houses can be problematic, there is a need for a staffed halfway house for women in NL.

A further complication in advocating for a halfway house for women in NL is that many women released from remand or provincial prisons would not qualify for parole or a temporary absence that would enable them to go to a halfway house. Thus, the halfway house would be out of reach for these women, who still require housing. Given the complicated nature of a traditional halfway house instead, I suggest that what is needed is a hybrid model. The hybrid model would consist of elements of a halfway house that meet the needs of CSC and the NLCCW with the needs of women released without a TA or parole. Such an arrangement would allow women to be released from prison without the benefit of a temporary absence or parole into safe housing. A staffed supported housing arrangement could provide parole or temporary absence options while maintaining a harm-reduction and supportive philosophy. The staffed housing arrangement can work with CSC, provincial prison staff and released women to address slips back into drug/alcohol use through counselling and appropriate support. A supportive housing arrangement would enable women to transition back into the community, ensure supports are in place, and transition to independent housing while adhering to correctional agencies' needs for supervision.

One of the challenges to such a model is how it would be funded. A traditional halfway house is funded based on bed space, meaning that the halfway house is funded by either CSC or a provincial government based on how many beds are filled at a given time. This model works for men's facilities based on numbers. However, as female prisoners are fewer in number, there may be times when a house is not at capacity. This means that a model based on per capita funding challenges the ability of a halfway house for women to maintain programming and staffing. Furthermore, as I have suggested, a hybrid model means that not all women would be in the care of a CSC or a provincial prison. Therefore, an alternate funding arrangement must be considered to provide adequate, safe housing for women leaving prison.

In addition to the recommendation for a hybrid halfway house/safe housing option for women released from prison, I suggest a need for change when considering parole conditions for alcohol and drug use. Policymakers and the Parole Board need to understand that recovery from addiction includes slips and relapses back into drug use. We must consider how parole and halfway houses can support recovery rather than penalize a normal part of the recovery process. There seems to be some understanding from parole officers that parolees will slip or relapse on their journey towards recovery. For example, Ricciardelli and McKendy (2021) found that parole officers did not revoke/suspend paroled women right away after having been found using alcohol or drugs. Parole officers engaged parolees in a series of interventions, including therapeutic counselling, indicating that they understand that maintaining abstinence is not an easy process. However, that refraining from alcohol/drug use is a parole condition at all demonstrates a lack of understanding of the process of addiction. In having alcohol and drug restrictions in parole orders, the Parole Board criminalizes an activity that is not a crime (alcohol use/prescription medication misuse) and criminalizes a normal part of recovery; slips and relapse. As addressed in the next section, an understanding of harm-reduction approaches would benefit correctional service systems in supporting those with addiction issues.

Harm Reduction

Service providers spoke about the importance of a harm-reduction approach while working with criminalized women. Vivian, a service provider working for ten years, suggested that although a harm-reduction approach is essential, women accessing services do not necessarily know what programmes include such an approach. She stated that many women she works with believe that they cannot access services if they are under the influence of alcohol or drugs. However, this is not always the case. Thus, service providers need to be open and honest about their ability to work with people who are actively using drugs or alcohol.

A harm-reduction approach requires meeting clients "where they are," meaning that service providers recognize that some clients want to access services but may not be ready to stop using harmful substances or stop engaging in risky behaviour (MacMaster, 2004). While recognizing that some clients might not be ready to stop using substances is essential, it is also vital that support exists for those ready to change their substance use. Recognizing that some women are making changes in their substance use means creating safe, sober spaces. Therefore, some services may require that participants refrain from drug use. For example, a therapeutic addictions group where women are trying to change their substance use would require that women do not access the group while under the influence of substances. Having participants who appear under the influence attend such a group can be harmful to others in attendance as it can trigger cravings to use substances. At the same time, formerly incarcerated women need services such as drop-in and groups to access connections, support, and fundamental (tangible) services such as telephones, computers, and hygiene products, whereby sobriety may not be as important. Services that assist in finding housing can be more flexible around substance use and not require sobriety at the moment. On the other hand, other women are ready to engage in therapeutic work, whereby counselling appointments may be appropriate, and sobriety is required for the duration of that appointment.

A wide variety of women are accessing services with a wide variety of needs. In response, services need to be flexible and wide-ranging. For example, in her assessment of UK-based programming designed to provide "supported desistance" to criminalized women, Barr (2018) found that services needed to be relational and provided based on each individual's needs. Therefore, careful assessment of individual needs will require a harm-reduction approach. Such a flexible approach acknowledges the diversity of women who access services and consideration for what purpose.

SPECIALIZED SERVICES FOR CRIMINALIZED WOMEN

Interview participants suggest that women leaving prison and criminalized women, in general, need support and services. However, some service providers stated that women had expressed discomfort in being referred to an agency that only works with criminalized women. They suggest that a mixed group of women might decrease the stigma associated with programmes for criminalized women. While I agree that stigma can be associated with a criminal past and see the value of a mixed group, I question if criminalized women can get their needs met if programming becomes more open to those without a criminal history. Are women less likely to address an issue related to prison stays or a criminal lifestyle in a mixed group? For example, the Just Us Women's Centre, Stella's Circle in St John's, NL, was started due to a lack of services for this specific population, criminalized women. There are existing services for women, but a needs assessment revealed that criminalized women, in particular, were not having their specific needs met (Boland & Morton Ninomiya, 2009).

Given that criminalized women are a group that endures a great deal of stigma, I suggest that specialized services are needed that provide non-judgemental support. Furthermore, expertise in issues that impact criminalized women is needed. Understanding the criminal justice system, courts, parole and record suspension is required while supporting criminalized women. For example, women in the current study stated that they appreciated the services provided by the Just Us Women's Centre both in prison and community because the staff had an understanding of the justice system and the issues that criminalized women face. Furthermore, some women stated that they liked that other criminalized women at the Just Us Women's Centre were supportive, and they felt a sense of community.

On the other hand, service providers such as those at Just Us Women's Centre (and I count myself among them) also need to understand the nuances of desistance processes, including a rejection of identifying with other criminalized women. The idea that some women reject identifying with other criminalized women was a key learning for my social work practice. While I have certainly heard women state that they do not like other women, I did not connect their feelings to the desistance process whereby they may distance themselves from their criminal background. The new insight will impact my practice as I endeavour to create a safe and supportive environment for women to engage in their desistance processes.

ADDRESSING STRUCTURAL STIGMA

Structural stigma is inequity and injustice embedded in social institutions' rules, policies, and procedures, such as health care or the criminal justice system (Livingston, 2021). Structural stigma impacted women in my study who experienced difficulties obtaining employment and housing and challenges receiving supportive health care. Combating structural stigma is difficult. However, there is evidence that individuals and institutions can make strides to challenge the injustices embedded within our systems. For example, the Mental Health Commission of Canada has shared approaches addressing structural stigma in Canada (Knaak & Sukhera, 2021). One such example is a multi-disciplinary team within hospitals to help support patients with substance use concerns. Their approach involves education for staff as well as a patient-centred focus whereby the patient is a participant in their health care plan.

Many women in my study reported facing stigma in relation to their criminal history. Furthermore, they reported that they often turn the stigma from others inward to experience self-stigma and feelings of shame. In the current study, women reported feeling undeserving of support from others, meaning that desistance processes were impeded because women felt that they could not access the services needed. Enhancing self-esteem and self-empowerment can reduce the negative impacts of self-stigma (Evans et al., 2018). Therefore, service providers can help women combat self-stigma by encouraging positive activities and achievements. For example, Evans and colleagues (2018) found that educational achievement while in prison reduced self-sigma and enhanced motivation to move away from the self-fulfilling attitude that accompanies self-stigma (i.e., once a criminal, always a criminal). Likewise, researchers have found that arts-based programmes offered in prisons enhance feelings of empowerment, self-esteem, and confidence (Brown & Lewis, 2004; Merrill & Frigon, 2015; Nugent & Loucks, 2011) and have the potential to assist prisoners in moving through the process of desistance (Sheppard & Ricciardelli, 2016; Windsor & Sheppard, 2023).

Building on the idea of helping women explore achievements through education or arts, I turn to Maruna's (2011) thoughts about rituals and how rituals can assist with reintegration. Maruna (2011) argues that rituals serve a purpose in society: to create solidarity. Lacking in reintegration processes is a familiar ritual that may create a sense of solidarity throughout the reintegration process. Unlike punishment, where there are many familiar rituals, such as court or prison, Maruna (2011) asks what would be needed to develop rituals of reintegration powerful enough to counteract the degradation of punishment. He states that contemporary Western societies have been poor at reintegrating and re-accepting people who have committed crimes back into society. Thus, rituals for rites of passage could be a valuable means to bring people back into communities. He suggests that reintegration rituals could include symbolic and emotive acts such as expressions of remorse from the person who committed a crime and messages of hope to that person from the community. Rituals must involve the community, emphasizing a community of care, not just professionals or volunteers, but the public to witness as there is often no media to show reintegration. Maruna (2011) suggests shifting from a focus on risk to looking at challenges and achievement. Focusing on rituals related to achievements is where I see possibilities for rehabilitation. Service providers can incorporate rituals into existing programming, emphasizing hope for the future. We can support criminalized women with some measure of public exposure about their redemption. I am not proposing that individual women need to share their stories of redemption publicly. However, I suggest that service providers and academics anonymously share women's stories of redemption in public ways to reduce stigma.

Reflecting on My Social Work Practice

My wish to help the criminalized women I work with daily drives the current study. I want to understand how women view their processes of working towards desistance. Not all women I work with are ready to make significant changes. However, I want to help those ready to do so while supporting women not ready for change, hoping they have a trusting relationship with me when and if they are ready for change. Therefore, I examine how the present research has impacted my professional social work practice in the current section.

To begin, I see a need to balance between personal and structural reasons for desistance. Feminist criminologists have been critical of how prison programming targets the individual, making her responsible for choices without recognizing the context in which she makes those choices (Barr, 2019). For example, Hart (2017) found that the responsibilization agenda has not fully been communicated to women, meaning that prison staff believed that women needed to participate in release planning by actively reaching out. However, women were waiting for available services to make contact with them. Thus, while there is an expectation of taking responsibility, women may not be aware of expectations. What is more, women in prison are used to being told what to do and thus may be reluctant to take an active role in their case planning.

In the current study, formerly incarcerated women spoke about their need to take responsibility for their actions and future. On the other hand, like feminist criminologists, service providers pointed out systemic issues at play that may impact women's choices. Service providers were critical of systems that did not provide adequate resources or understanding of women's lived realities. Women did identify issues such as housing, poverty, and sexism but still saw the solutions to these problems as in the realm of individual work. Women interviewed emphasized that they must reach out and "want it." On the other hand, service providers stated that we, the service providers, have to reach out to women.

As a social worker, I engage women at the individual level. Women come to me because they want to make a change and, in some cases, "take responsibility" because they have bought into the rhetoric of the criminal justice system. Women are struggling, sometimes, because of the choices they make. Sometimes, helping a shift in thinking or developing interpersonal skills can help make them more employable or help facilitate relationships with family. However, I also recognize that they make choices in contexts where choices are limited and may not be considered the right choice. I see that the system has to change. My role as a social worker is to advocate for that change. However, systems are slow to change. Therefore, we cannot dismiss women who say that they want their lives to be better because we operate in oppressive systems based on sex, class, and race, which can impede (but not entirely prevent) their ability to make changes in their lives. I have witnessed many women make positive, life-affirming changes in their lives! Therefore, as a service provider, I need to support personal agency within the larger systems that diminish criminalized women's opportunities for future growth.

For the women I interviewed, their ideas of personal responsibility for making change fit the desistance literature. Maruna's (2001) theory of desistance suggests that for a person to "go straight," they must generate a gradual shift in self-narrative. Those who can "rehabilitate" generate a positive self-narrative that states that they are still good people even though they have done wrong. Thus, within Maruna's framework for desistance, there is a great deal of emphasis on the work of the individual.

Indeed, there are systemic barriers, and it is my job both as a researcher and as a service provider to identify and mitigate barriers. However, I also need to listen to women telling me that they have a role to play. Maruna (2001) argues that an optimistic view of control over destiny is needed to engage in the desistance process. Given the importance of a sense of control over one's destiny, women's assertions that "you have to want it" and their belief in their abilities to make changes are crucial in the process of desistance.

I argue that service providers must acknowledge that a combination of issues is at play. Some desistance literature emphasizes the personal responsibility needed for change, but there needs to be an acknowledgement that the person's ability to change does not happen in a vacuum. Implications for service providers then are to work with women's ideas of personal responsibility while helping them see the systemic issues that will impact their journey towards a "better life." One such way of helping women see systemic issues can be "bearing witness" to the lived experience of criminalized women, seeking to understand their values, the meaning ascribed to criminal behaviour, and goals for the future (Anderson, 2016). With the knowledge gleaned from bearing witness to desisting and criminalized women, service providers can help at the individual level while advocating at the macro level. At the same time, women still need to do the work and take advantage of opportunities, such as employment or the development of pro-social relationships. Thus, service providers can support women in doing the work of change while helping women seek out growth opportunities.

The research process has helped me shift my practice as I have engaged with my research data over the last few years. I have been more aware of "change talk" that hints at the process of desistance. For example, when talking to women in prison about their criminal activities, they will often say, "That's not me." Before researching desistance, this was a confusing sentiment and easily misconstrued as "not taking responsibility" for past actions. However, now I can see these words hint at desistance whereby a woman separates herself from a past criminal lifestyle. Interpreting women's words through a desistance lens can help allow me to support that desistance process. After hearing that the criminal acts are "not me," I can shift a conversation to a discussion of the "real person" and help them to uncover the core beliefs that characterize "true self," and a desire to be productive and give back to society (Maruna, 2001).

References

Anderson, S. E. (2016). The value of 'bearing witness' to desistance. *Probation Journal, 63*(4), 408–424.

Barr, Ú. (2018). Gendered assisted desistance: A decade from Corston. *Safer Communities, 17*(2), 81–93.

Barr, Ú. (2019). *Desisting sisters*. Springer.

Boland, B., & Morton Ninomiya, M. (2009). *Time better spent: Seeking justice for women in the criminal justice system*. Stella's Circle.

Brown, J., & Lewis, S. (2004). An evaluation of dancing inside: A creative workshop project led by Motionhouse Dance Theatre in HMP Dovegate therapeutic community, year two programme. *Two-year programme. Forensic Psychology Research Unit, Surrey University*. Retrieved March 2, 2024, from http://www.artsevidence.org.uk/media/uploads/evaluation-downloads/mh-surrey-yr2-2004.pdf

Evans, D. N., Pelletier, E., & Szkola, J. (2018). Education in prison and the self-stigma: Empowerment continuum. *Crime & Delinquency, 64*(2), 255–280.

Foucault, M. (1995). *Discipline and punish: The birth of prison*. Vintage.

Hart, E. L. (2017). Women prisoners and the drive for desistance: Capital and responsibilization as a barrier to change. *Women & Criminal Justice, 27*(3), 151–169.

Knaak, S., & Sukhera, J. (2021). *Real-world examples of approaches that address mental illness- and substance use-related structural stigma in Canada's health-care system*. Mental Health Commission of Canada.

Livingston, J. D. (2021). *A framework for assessing structural stigma in health-care: Contexts for people with mental health and substance use issues*. Mental Health Commission of Canada.

MacMaster, S. (2004). Harm reduction: A new perspective on substance abuse services. *Social Work, 49*(3), 356–363.

Maier, K. (2020a). Canada's 'open prisons': Hybridisation and the role of halfway houses in penal scholarship and practice. *The Howard Journal of Crime and Justice, 59*(4), 381–399.

Maier, K. (2020b). Intermediary workers: Narratives of supervision and support work within the halfway house setting. *Probation Journal, 67*(4), 410–426.

Maruna, S. (2001). *Making good: How ex-convicts reform and rebuild their lives*. American Psychological Association.

Maruna, S. (2011). Reentry as a rite of passage. *Punishment & Society, 13*(1), 3–28.

McKendy, L., & Ricciardelli, R. (2020). The pains of release: Federally-sentenced women's experiences on parole. *European Journal of Probation*, 1–20.

Merrill, E., & Frigon, S. (2015). Performative criminology and the "state of play" for theatre with criminalized women. *Societies, 5*(2), 295–313.

Nugent, B., & Loucks, N. (2011). The arts and prisoners: Experiences of creative rehabilitation. *The Howard Journal of Criminal Justice, 50*(4), 356–370.

Opsal, T. (2012). 'Livin' on the straights': Identity, desistance, and work among women post-incarceration. *Sociological Inquiry, 82*(3), 378–403.

Reiter, K. (2014). Making windows in walls: Strategies for prison research. *Qualitative Inquiry, 20*(4), 417–428.

Ricciardelli, R., & McKendy, L. (2021). A qualitative analysis of parole suspensions among women on parole. *Canadian Journal of Criminology and Criminal Justice, 63*(1), 89–105.

Sheppard, A., & Ricciardelli, R. (2016). Let's dance: Exploring dance programs in prisons in the context of reentry. *Journal of Community Corrections, 25*(4), 9–15.

Travis, J. (2002). Invisible punishment: An instrument of social exclusion. In M. Mauer & M. Chesney-Lind (Eds.), *Invisible punishment: The collateral consequences of mass imprisonment* (pp. 15–36). New Press.

Windsor, K., & Sheppard, A. (2023). Dance as revolution: Exploring prisoner agency through arts-based methods in prison. *Journal of Studies in Social Justice, 17*(2), 222–240.

CHAPTER 7

Conclusion

Abstract In this chapter, I summarize the cognitive processes of women engaged in the desistance process. Drug and alcohol use impact the desistance process. In addition, systemic barriers impact women's ability to commit to a crime-free life. Nevertheless, women continue to engage in desistance processes and with supports from service providers, they can meet their life goals.

Keywords Agency · Desistance · Service providers · Addiction

The women I interviewed for this project are engaged in the desistance process, and their experiences fit within aspects of theoretical frameworks used to describe desistance. For most women interviewed, drug and alcohol use is a significant factor in criminal activity. Moreover, women would define themselves as having an addiction rather than characterizing themselves as merely misusing substances. For women in the current study, addiction means a lack of control over their alcohol/drug use, leading to a lack of control in all aspects of life, including criminal activity. Women engaged in the desistance process by exercising some measure of control over their lives. However, the key to that control was addressing their addiction.

Women have engaged in cognitive processes associated with desistance. Again, they state, "You have to want it," meaning that the individual needs to commit to a change in lifestyle and that no amount of help or support will compel someone to make a change without their own will. However, given the intense levels of addiction of the women interviewed, they have also shared that they could not think, in other words, engage in a cognitive process until going to prison forced them to detox. Thus, desistance is a complicated process for women whereby one's will can be clouded by substance use. However, women state that will and desire to change is essential in making changes in substance use and, therefore, criminal activity.

Nevertheless, women can engage in a desistance process, even when social harms and barriers remain. For some women, their connection to services such as Emmanuel House and the Just Us Women's Centre mitigates some social barriers. These services can provide access to safe, secure housing, community connections, and some concrete help that can help supplement income, such as food, clothing, and hygiene products. However, large-scale systemic barriers remain. In the face of systemic barriers, women engaged in the desistance process, citing their agency as the means to do so: repeatedly, women stated, "You have to want it." For many women, changing a criminal lifestyle and moving towards a new, pro-social lifestyle means dealing with their addiction issues and abstaining from drugs or alcohol. For all women, moving towards desistance means accessing support through professionals and informal means such as friends and peer networks. However, they are clear; they must do the work, including making a cognitive shift moving towards pro-social behaviours and a vision of a new self.

Given the evidence provided by formerly incarcerated women and services providers interviewed for the current study, I argue that understanding provincially sentenced women's desistance must include both a theory of cognitive transformation and an approach to understanding the social conditions in which women live. Resulting from these interviews is a discussion of what women say they need to support their desistance process: adequate housing on release, transportation, and support for mental health and addiction issues. They need services that are in tune with their lives, suggesting services need to be gender and trauma-responsive. In general, most women thought that the services provided in prison were good quality but that there were not enough of them, suggesting a need for more contact with counsellors and support in release planning. Furthermore, women stated that there are good quality services in the community. However, service providers need to promote better what is available and perhaps increase the number of hours women have access to service providers and the associated services.

On the other hand, service providers were more likely to identify systemic issues that barred women from achieving their goals of a crime-free lifestyle. Service providers identified long waitlists, problematic policies, and systemic difficulties like poverty and racism. In general, service providers believe that the system needs to change to meet women's needs. In contrast, formerly incarcerated women spoke about their responsibility to access services. Thus, to support women's desistance, I argue in favour of a partnership between service providers supporting criminalized women and criminalized women themselves. Women can take responsibility for working towards desistance, and the role of service providers is to support individual changes but also to identify and advocate for change to systemic barriers.

The desistance process can be challenging. However, women in my study could successfully engage in desistance for long periods. At the time of this writing, only one woman returned to prison. Some women in the current study have desisted for years, while others were beginning their journey. It is a challenging process for formerly incarcerated women, and it is also a challenging process for service providers supporting these women. Information from women can be contradictory. For example, some women stated that they did not like other women, and some stated that they did not want to be around men. These sentiments often came from the same women! People are contradictory. They often change opinions from moment to moment based on what is happening at that time. Women's changing opinions do not mean that women do not know what they need or want, but it means that needs and wants change and are complicated.

So what are service providers to do? The best we can. We can help where and when we can. We can offer a wide variety of services, recognizing the heterogeneity of women. We can help people to resolve some of the barriers they place on themselves. We can recognize systemic issues and advocate to make changes to systems. As a formerly incarcerated woman, Laura stated, "Nobody's going to come knocking at your door and ask if you need help. No, that's not going to happen. Right? Yeah, you gotta be able to at least make a phone call." Service providers need to be there to answer the call.

INDEX

© The Editor(s) (if applicable) and The Author(s), under exclusive license to Springer Nature Switzerland AG 2024
A. Sheppard, *Life on The Outside*,
https://doi.org/10.1007/978-3-031-63817-6

114   INDEX

GPSR Compliance

The European Union's (EU) General Product Safety Regulation (GPSR) is a set of rules that requires consumer products to be safe and our obligations to ensure this.

If you have any concerns about our products, you can contact us on ProductSafety@springernature.com

In case Publisher is established outside the EU, the EU authorized representative is:

Springer Nature Customer Service Center GmbH
Europaplatz 3
69115 Heidelberg, Germany

The manufacturer's authorised representative in the EU is Springer
Nature Customer Service Centre GmbH, Europaplatz 3, 69115 Heidelberg,
Germany. If you have any concerns regarding our products, please
contact ProductSafety@springernature.com

Printed and bound by CPI Group (UK) Ltd, Croydon, CR0 4YY
29/04/2026
02099531-0005